Microsoft® Project For Windows™

Version 3

Step by Step

Catapult

Microsoft PRESS

PUBLISHED BY
Microsoft Press
A Division of Microsoft Corporation
One Microsoft Way
Redmond, Washington 98052-6399

Copyright © 1993 by Catapult, Inc.

Library of Congress Cataloging-in-Publication Data
Microsoft Project for Windows step by step / Catapult, Inc.
       p.   cm.
   Includes index.
   ISBN 1-55615-523-9
    1. Microsoft Project for Windows.   2. Industrial project
management--Computer programs.   I. Catapult, Inc.
HD69.P75M534 1992
658.4'04'0285543--dc20   92-23781
                                 CIP

Printed and bound in the United States of America.

3 4 5 6 7 8 9 MLML 7 6 5 4 3 2

Distributed to the book trade in Canada by Macmillan of Canada, a division of Canada Publishing Corporation.

Distributed to the book trade outside the United States and Canada by Penguin Books Ltd.

Penguin Books Ltd., Harmondsworth, Middlesex, England
Penguin Books Australia Ltd., Ringwood, Victoria, Australia
Penguin Books N.Z. Ltd., 182-190 Wairau Road, Auckland 10, New Zealand

British Cataloging-in-Publication Data available.

Microsoft, MS, and MS-DOS are registered trademarks and Windows and the Windows operating system logo are trademarks of Microsoft Corporation.

Companies, names, and/or data used in screens and sample output are fictitious unless otherwise noted.

The Catapult, Inc. Curriculum Development Group
Editor: Gregory G. Schultz
Associate Editor: Donald Elman
Writer: Marie L. Swanson

Contents

Part 1   Learning the Basics

Appendixes

About This Book

Microsoft Project is a powerful project management application that you can use for planning, scheduling, and charting project information for project management, as well as for presenting project information to others. *Microsoft Project Step by Step* is a tutorial that shows you how to use Microsoft Project to simplify your work and increase your productivity. You can use *Microsoft Project Step by Step* in a classroom setting, or you can use it as a tutorial to learn Microsoft Project at your own pace and at your own convenience.

You also get hands-on practice using the files on the accompanying disk. Instructions for copying the practice files to your computer's hard disk are in "Getting Ready," the next section in this book.

Finding the Best Starting Point for You

This book is designed for new users learning Microsoft Project for the first time, and for experienced users who want to learn and use the new features in Microsoft Project version 3. Even if you are a novice user, *Microsoft Project Step by Step* will help you get the most out of Microsoft Project.

The modular design of this book offers you considerable flexibility in customizing your learning. Lesson 1 provides an overview of project management principles and concepts. Lesson 2 teaches basic skills for using Microsoft Project.

The table at the start of each lesson will help you decide if you want to complete a particular lesson. You can work through the lessons in any order, skip lessons, and repeat lessons later to brush up on certain skills. Each lesson builds on concepts presented in previous lessons, so you may want to back up if you find that you don't understand some concepts or terminology.

This book is divided into five major parts, each containing several related lessons. At the end of each part, you will find a Review & Practice section that gives you the opportunity to practice the skills you learned in that part. In this less-structured example, you can test your knowledge and prepare for your own projects.

You start most lessons by opening a practice file from the WINPROJ\PRACTICE directory on your hard disk. You then rename the practice file so that the original file remains unchanged while you work on your own version. This allows you, or another learner, to reuse the original files.

Use the following table to determine your best first step.

If you are	Follow these steps
New to a computer or graphical environment, such as Microsoft Windows	Read "Getting Ready," the next section in this book. Next, work through Lessons 1 and 2. Work through the other lessons in any order.
New to the mouse	Read "If You Are New to Using the Mouse" in "Getting Ready," the next section in this book. Follow the instructions for installing the practice files in the "Getting Ready" section in this book. Next, work through Lessons 1 and 2. Work through the other lessons in any order.
Familiar with a graphical computer environment but new to project management and Microsoft Project	Follow the instructions for installing the practice files in the "Getting Ready" section in this book. Next, work through Lessons 1 and 2. Work through the other lessons in any order.
Familiar with a graphical computer environment and project management, but new to Microsoft Project	Follow the instructions for installing the practice files in the "Getting Ready" section in this book. Next, work through Lesson 2. Work through the other lessons in any order.

Using This Book as a Classroom Aid

If you're an instructor, you can use Microsoft Project Step by Step for teaching Microsoft Project to novice users. You may want to select certain lessons that meet your students' needs and incorporate your own demonstrations into the lessons.

If you plan to teach the entire contents of this book, you should probably set aside two full days of classroom time to allow for discussion, questions, and any customized practice you may create.

Conventions Used in This Book

Before you start any of the lessons, it's important that you understand the terms and notational conventions used in this book.

Notational Conventions

- Characters you are to type appear in **bold**.
- Important terms and titles of books appear in *italic*.

Procedural Conventions

- Procedures you are to follow are given in numbered lists (1, 2, and so on). A triangular bullet (▶) indicates a procedure with only one step.

- The word *choose* is used for carrying out a command from either a menu or a command button.

- The word *select* is used for highlighting fields, text, and menu or command names, and for selecting options in a dialog box.

Mouse Conventions

- If you have a multiple-button mouse, Microsoft Project assumes that you have configured the left mouse button as the primary mouse button. Any procedure that requires you to click the secondary button will refer to it as the right mouse button.

- *Click* means to point to an object and then press and release the mouse button. For example, "Click the Cut button on the tool bar."

- *Drag* means to press and hold the mouse button while you move the mouse. For example, "Drag from task 1 through task 8."

- *Double-click* means to rapidly press and release the mouse button twice. For example, "Double-click the Microsoft Project icon to start Microsoft Project."

  You can adjust the mouse tracking speed and double-click speed in Control Panel. For more information, see your system documentation.

Keyboard Conventions

- Names of keys are in small capital letters—for example, TAB and SHIFT.

- You can choose commands with the keyboard. Press the ALT key to activate the menu bar; then press the keys for the underlined letters in the menu name and the command name. For some commands, you can press the key combination listed in the menu.

- A plus sign (+) between two key names means that you must press those keys at the same time. For example, "Press SHIFT+SPACEBAR" means that you hold down the SHIFT key while you press the spacebar.

Other Features of This Book

Cut button

- You can perform many commands by clicking a button on the tool bar. When a procedure instructs you to click a button, a picture of the button appears in the left margin, as the Cut button does here.

- Text in the left margin gives tips, additional useful information, or keyboard alternatives.

- The optional "One Step Further" exercises at the end of the lesson are less structured, and present operations that you can carry out to apply what you learned in the lesson.

- At the end of each major part of the book, there is a Review & Practice section where you can practice the skills you learned in that part.

Cross-References to Microsoft Project Documentation

References to the *Microsoft Project User's Reference, Microsoft Project Features Guide,* and online tutorial lessons throughout this book help acquaint you with other sources of helpful information. Using the references to these sources will help you make greater use of the features in Microsoft Project.

Help

Microsoft Project Help provides online information about Microsoft Project features and gives instructions for performing specific tasks. You will learn more about Help in Getting Ready, the next section in this book.

Online Tutorial

The Microsoft Project online tutorial contains information about the features in Microsoft Project and teaches the basic skills you need to become productive in Microsoft Project. It also provides overviews and hands-on practice for each of the main parts of the application. In Microsoft Project, you can go through the tutorials with either the mouse or the keyboard.

You will learn how to run the tutorial in Getting Ready, the next section in this book.

Microsoft Project Features Guide

This manual provides a brief overview of project management terms and concepts, plus general descriptions of Microsoft Project features and functions. Review this book to get a general idea of the capabilities you can take advantage of in Microsoft Project.

Microsoft Project User's Reference

This extensive manual is an alphabetical reference providing comprehensive information and detailed instructions for using all of the functions and options in Microsoft Project. Use it whenever you want more information about a particular topic covered in a lesson.

Getting Ready

By completing the lessons in this book, you will learn how to organize and create project plans using Microsoft Project. This book also shows you how to use the features in this powerful program to manage projects and communicate results.

Each lesson is estimated to take approximately 45 minutes or less. You can set your own pace according to your personal learning style and experience level. Every lesson ends with a short exercise called "One Step Further."

Installing the Step by Step Practice Files

Included with this book is a disk called "Practice Files for Microsoft Project Step by Step." These files are copied to your hard disk into a new directory named PRACTICE under the WINPROJ directory. A special program on the Practice Files disk automatically installs these files for you.

Copy the practice files to your hard disk

1 Turn on your computer.

2 Insert the Practice Files disk into drive A of your computer.

   In some computers, the drive that matches the Practice Files disk might be drive B. If so, substitute "drive B" for each reference to drive A.

3 At the MS-DOS command prompt (usually "C:\"), type **A:INSTALL**

   Do not type a space between "A:" and "INSTALL." If you are using drive B, replace "A:" with "B:".

4 Follow the instructions on the screen.

   You can press ESC at any time to exit the practice file installation program.

Protecting Existing Microsoft Project Configuration

Important Installing practice files standardizes the appearance of your Microsoft Project screen and calendar. These instructions are needed only if you want to preserve changes you may have made that customize the appearance or arrangement of the Microsoft Project screen or calendar.

To ensure that you get results that match those in the lessons, and to protect customized view and calendar files (and projects associated with them) from being affected by any changes made during the lessons, you should temporarily rename the default view and calendar files. When you are finished using this book, you can easily restore the previous customized appearance.

Other changes to the appearance of your projects can be made with the Preferences command in the Options menu. To ensure results that match these lessons, you need to reset the Preferences dialog box manually.

Appendix B contains step-by-step instructions for renaming your current view and calendar files, and later restoring them to their original condition. It also contains instructions for resetting the Preferences dialog box. If you have customized the appearance of Microsoft Project, you should follow these instructions before beginning the lessons in *Microsoft Project Step by Step*.

Using the Practice Files

When you work with Microsoft Project, you store project information in *project files*. As you work through the lessons using the practice project files, be sure to follow the instructions for renaming the project files. By modifying the file names, you can make changes, experiment, and observe results in your own version of the project file, and later reuse the original files if you wish.

Because each lesson begins with a fresh practice file, be sure to close your current project file and open a new one before you begin a new lesson. Using a practice file from another lesson may not give you the results you expect; what you see may be different from what is shown in the lessons.

Lesson Scenario

For these lessons, imagine that you are the operations manager for Victory Sports, Inc., a sporting goods distributor. The lease is up for your office and warehouse, and your company wants to move to a larger facility. You need to organize the move of 100 workers and a completely full warehouse. Throughout these lessons, you will use Microsoft Project to assist you in managing the project.

Types of Lesson Files

The table below lists and describes the types of project file names used in this book.

This type of file name	Is used in this way
PRACT*nn*.MPP	The general form of file names used in each lesson. In each actual file name, the characters *nn* are replaced by a two-digit number or code corresponding to the lesson or appendix number (for example, 03 for Lesson 3, and XA for Appendix A). The extension MPP is used by Microsoft Project for all project files. If more than one file is used in a lesson, the file number (*nn*) is followed by a sequence letter (A, B, etc.).
*n*ANNUAL.MPP	The form for file names used in each Review & Practice section. In this case, *n* is a single digit referring to the Review & Practice Part number.

This type of file name	Is used in this way
SBSMORE.MPV	In Microsoft Project, a file with the extension MPV is called a view file. You will learn more about view files in Lesson 2.
MONTHLY.MPV	A view file used in Lesson 18.

Starting Microsoft Project

After you install Microsoft Project and copy the practice project files to your hard disk, you can start the application.

Starting Microsoft Project for Windows

Use the following procedures to start Windows and Microsoft Project. Your screen may be different from the following illustrations, depending on your particular setup and the applications installed on your computer. For more information about Windows, see the *Microsoft Windows User's Guide*.

Start Windows from the MS-DOS command prompt

1   At the system prompt, type **win**

2   Press ENTER.

After the initial startup, the Program Manager window looks like the following illustration. You can start all of your applications, including Microsoft Project, from Program Manager.

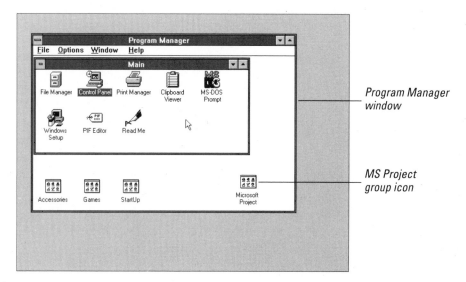

Program Manager window

MS Project group icon

When Windows is active, everything on your screen (called the *desktop*) is displayed in a *window*. You can adjust each window to the size you want and you can move windows anywhere you want on the desktop. You can have multiple windows open at the same time to compare and share information easily.

The Program Manager window   Within the Program Manager window are symbols that represent applications and documents. These symbols, called *icons,* are used to open the applications they represent. The icons are organized in groups, usually related to applications. The default installation of Microsoft Project creates a group named Microsoft Project.You use these icons to open the applications they represent.

The Microsoft Project group   Double-clicking the Microsoft Project group icon opens the Microsoft Project program group window. This window contains the icons for Microsoft Project and its related applications.

As you become more familiar with Windows, you will find that you can customize the startup screen to your personal working style.

Start Microsoft Project for Windows

1   Double-click the Microsoft Project group icon.

     This opens Microsoft Project program group.

2   Double-click the Microsoft Project program icon.

Using the Online Tutorial

Microsoft Project includes an online tutorial that covers both an overview of how to use Windows and an introduction to the basics of project management. There are also demonstrations of many of the features in Microsoft Project. Hands-on activities give you a chance to practice using the application.

There is a general match between the lessons in this book and the lessons in the online tutorial. One effective way to use the tutorial is to run a tutorial lesson related to the features in the *Step by Step* lesson you have just completed. In this way, the tutorial can be an excellent review. Similarly, you can run a tutorial lesson covering the topics in an upcoming lesson. This is a good way to preview new skills.

Run the Microsoft Project online tutorial

1   From the Help menu, choose Tutorial.

2   From the Main Menu, select a lesson.

3   Follow the instructions on the screen.

4   To quit the tutorial, choose the Exit button.

If You Are New to Windows

Windows is designed for both ease of use and sophistication of function. It helps you handle virtually all of the daily work that you carry out with your computer. Windows provides a common basis among different application programs—both in the way they share data and in the way you control their operations.

Once you become familiar with the basic elements of Windows, you can apply these skills to learn and use Microsoft Project, as well as many other types of applications, including word processing, graphics, or spreadsheets.

Using Windows Applications

When you start Microsoft Project, it opens a new project called Project1. The next project you create is called Project2, and so on. You can rename a project when you save it. Each project is displayed in a window.

The project window in Microsoft Project looks like the following illustration.

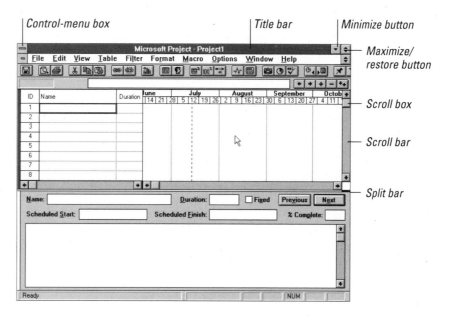

You can scroll, move, split, and close a window by using the mouse.

To	Do this
Scroll through a window (to see another part of the project)	Click the scroll bars or drag the scroll box.
Change the size of a window	Drag any of the window edges or corners.

To	Do this
Enlarge a window to fill the screen	Double-click the title bar or click the Maximize button.
Restore a window to its previous size	Click the Restore button.
Move a window	Drag the title bar.
Split a window	Drag the split box on the scroll bar to where you want the split.
Close a window	Double-click the Control-menu box.

Quitting Microsoft Project and Windows

If you would like to quit Microsoft Project, follow these steps to exit the program.

Quit Microsoft Project

1   Hold down the ALT key and press F4.

2   If you see a message box asking whether you want to save your work, choose the Yes button.

If you have just quit Microsoft Project and would like to quit Windows, here is a simple way to exit from Windows.

Quit Windows

1   Hold down the ALT key and press F4.

2   When you see a box with the message, "This will end your Windows session," press ENTER.

Understanding Microsoft Project Menus and Commands

In Microsoft Project, menus and commands behave according to Microsoft Windows conventions. Menu names appear in the *menu bar*, across the top of the screen. A list of commands appears when you click on a menu name in the menu bar. To choose a command, click the menu name and then click the command on the list.

The following illustration shows the Microsoft Project menu bar with the Edit menu displayed.

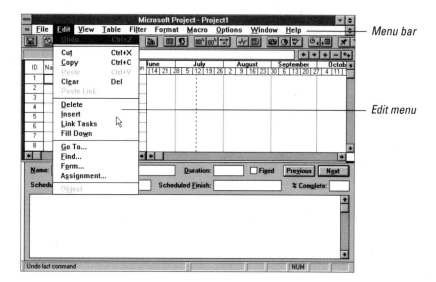

Some commands have a *shortcut key* combination listed to the right of the command name. Once you are familiar with the menus and commands, these shortcut keys can save you time.

When a command name appears dimmed, it doesn't apply to your current situation or is unavailable. For example, the Paste command on the Edit menu appears dimmed if the Copy or Cut command has not been used first.

The list of commands in a menu can change depending on the type of project information displayed in the active window. For example, if the active window is a Task Form, the Format menu contains one list of commands. However, if the active window is a Gantt Chart, the Format menu contains a different list of commands.

When a command name displays a check mark to its left, the command is already in effect. For example, when you open the View menu, a check mark appears next to the name of the active view.

To close a menu without choosing a command, click the menu name again.

Using the Tool Bar

Save button

Located below the menu bar is the *tool bar* (sometimes called *Toolbar*). It contains buttons that are shortcuts for choosing commands and for working with Microsoft Project. For example, clicking the Save button on the tool bar is the same as choosing the Save command from the File menu.

Although initially you might feel more comfortable using the keyboard for making menu selections, it is generally much faster to click a button on the tool bar. The instructions in this book emphasize using the tool bar for almost all Microsoft Project operations. For data entry activities, however, both techniques are described so that you can decide for yourself which is faster.

Understanding Dialog Boxes

When you need to supply information for a command to proceed, a *dialog box* appears on the screen. After you enter information or make selections in the dialog box, click the OK button with the mouse or press the ENTER key to carry out the command. Choose the Cancel button or press ESC to close a dialog box and cancel an entry.

When you choose a command name that is followed by an ellipsis (. . .), Microsoft Project always displays a dialog box so that you can provide more information. Depending on the dialog box, you type the information or select from a group of options.

For example, the Page Setup dialog box is displayed when you choose the Page Setup command from the File menu. In the dialog box, you specify the characteristics you want for the pages in your project.

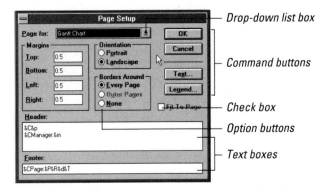

Dialog boxes are made up of a number of standard features:

Command buttons   You choose a command button to carry out an action. Choose the OK button to carry out a command, or choose the Cancel button to cancel a command.

Help buttons   If a Help button appears, choose it for more detailed assistance with dialog box procedures. Dialog boxes containing error messages usually contain a Help button to provide assistance with the problem.

Text boxes   Type information in a text box. Click the mouse in the box or tab until an insertion point appears in the box; then type your entry.

List boxes   Available choices are listed in a list box. If the list is longer than the box, you can use the scroll bar to see the rest of the list.

Drop-down list boxes An arrow at its right end identifies a drop-down list box. Selecting the arrow opens a list of available choices.

Option buttons   You can select only one option at a time from a group of option buttons. A selected option button has a black dot in its center.

Check boxes   You select check boxes to choose options that can be combined with one another, so you can select more than one at a time.

Selecting Dialog Box Options

To move around in a dialog box, click the item you want. You can also hold down ALT and press the key for the underlined letter at the same time. You can also press TAB to move between items.

Use the procedures in this table to select options in a dialog box with the mouse.

To	Do this
Select or clear an option button	Click the option button.
Select or clear a check box	Click the check box.
Select an item in a list box	Click the item. If the item is not visible, scroll through the list until you see it.
Select an item in a drop-down list box	Click the arrow to the right of the text box to display the drop-down list and select as from a normal list box.
Move to a text box	Click the text box.
Select text in a text box	Double-click a word or drag through the characters.
Scroll through a list box	Use the scroll bar.

After selecting the options you want, click the OK button or press ENTER to carry out the command. To cancel the command, click the Cancel button or press ESC.

Using Online Help

Microsoft Project includes Help, a complete online reference. You can get Help information in several ways.

To get Help information	Do this
By topic or activity	Choose Contents from the Help menu.
While working in a dialog box	Press F1.
While a message box is displayed	Choose the Help button.

Display the list of Help topics

▶ From the Help menu, choose Index.

A topic with the heading "Microsoft Project Help Index" appears.

The Help Index topic looks like the following illustration.

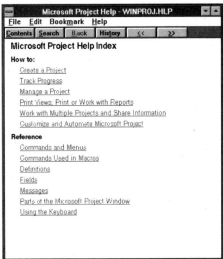

Clicking an underlined term "jumps" you to a related topic. Choosing the Back button in the Help window returns you to the previous Help topic.

Like all the windows in Microsoft Project, you can move, size, and scroll through a Help window. You can switch between the Help window and your document, or you can arrange the windows side by side so that you can refer to Help while you work.

Getting Help on Help

To learn how you can take advantage of all the information available in Help, choose the How to Use Help command from the Help menu.

Learn to use Help

1   From the Help menu, choose the How to Use Help command.

The Contents for How to Use Help looks like the following illustration.

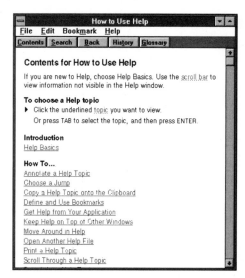

2 Click the word "topic," which has a dotted underline.

When you click a word that has a dotted underline, you get a box containing the definition of that word. A definition box looks like the following illustration.

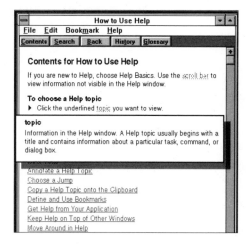

3 Click anywhere in the window to remove the definition box.

4 Under How To.., click the underlined text <u>Print a Help Topic</u>.

When you click text which has a solid underline, you get the Help topic for that subject. The next Help window looks like the following illustration.

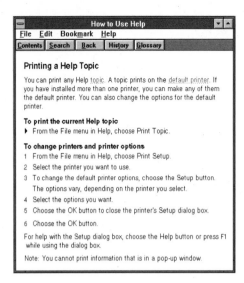

5 Choose the Contents button to return to the Contents for How to Use Help topic.

6 From the File menu, choose Exit.

Getting Help on Microsoft Project Topics

The Search command allows you to quickly locate help topics by using a key word. If you know the command or term you want help on, you can go directly to the topic.

Search for a topic

1 Press F1 to display the Help window.

2 Choose the Search button.

3 In the Search dialog box, type **views**

This is the key word which will be searched for.

4 When a list of topics appears, scroll through the list and select views: Gantt Charts

5 Choose the Show Topics button.

The search dialog box looks like the following illustration.

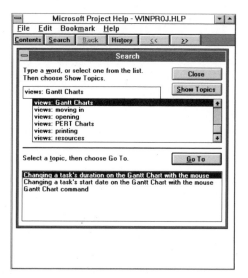

6 From the list of topics, select Gantt Chart command.

7 Choose the Go To button.

Microsoft project displays the Help topic for the Gantt Chart command.

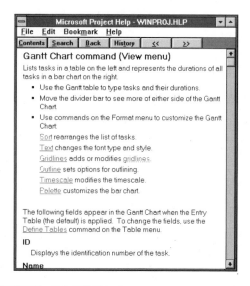

Note   You will encounter the Gantt Chart throughout Project. This is a help topic worth pausing to read now.

8 When you are through, double-click the Control-menu box in the upper left corner of the Help window to close Help.

If You Are New to Using the Mouse

Tool bars, shortcut menus, and many other features of Microsoft Project were designed for working with the mouse. Although you can use the keyboard for most actions in Microsoft Project, many of these actions are easier to do with the mouse.

Mouse Pointers

The mouse controls a pointer on the screen. You move the pointer by sliding the mouse over a flat surface in the direction you want the pointer to move. If you run out of room to move the mouse, lift it up and put it down again. The pointer moves only when the mouse is touching the flat surface.

Moving the mouse pointer across the screen does not affect the document; the pointer simply indicates a location on the screen. When you press the mouse button, something happens at the location of the pointer.

When the mouse pointer passes over different parts of the Microsoft Project window, it changes shape, indicating what it will do at that point. The following mouse pointers are examples of those you will see as you work in this book.

This pointer	Appears when you point to
⊳	The menu bar and tool bars to choose a command or a button, the title bar to move a window, and the scroll bars to scroll through a document.
⟷	A column heading boundary to change column width.
⟺	A split box on the scroll bar to split a window vertically.
☝	A button on a worksheet or a term in a Help topic that you can click to go to another topic.
I	A text box, or any area where characters can be entered from the keyboard.

Using the Mouse

These are the four basic mouse actions that you use throughout the lessons in this book.

Pointing   Moving the mouse to place the pointer on an item is called *pointing*.

Clicking   Pointing to an item on your screen and then quickly pressing and releasing the mouse button is called *clicking*. You select items on the screen and move around in a document by clicking.

Double-clicking   Pointing to an item and then quickly pressing and releasing the mouse button twice is called *double-clicking*. This is a convenient shortcut for many tasks in Microsoft Project.

Dragging   Holding down the mouse button as you move the pointer is called *dragging*. You can use this technique to select data in the rows and columns in tables.

Try the mouse

Take a moment to test drive the mouse. Just slide the mouse so that the pointer moves around the Microsoft Project screen.

1   Slide the mouse until the pointer is over the menus and tools at the top of the screen. The pointer is a left-pointing arrow.

2   Slide the mouse around the document window, the large open area in the center of the screen.

The document window is the area in which you work with the text on a project. The pointer looks like a large plus sign.

3   Slide the mouse pointer over the entry bar, above the project.

The pointer looks like an I-beam.

Part 1

Learning the Basics

Understanding Project Management Basics

What does it take to plan a project?

After you determine the project goals, all you have to do is figure out what steps are required, and who will do them, taking into account personal schedules. And when they will start. And when they will finish. And how much it could cost. Of course, once the project is under way, you have to answer a lot of questions about how the project is going. And adjust the schedule when the unexpected happens. And communicate with others so everyone works together. And....

You get the idea. Managing a project can be a full-time job, and chances are you already have one of those.

The good news is that a methodical approach facilitates effective project management. With your personal computer and convenient tools like Microsoft Project, you have the power to use many established project management practices.

What is a Project?

A *project* is the sequence of steps related to achieving a goal. What makes a project different from what you do every day is that a project goal is a specific, nonroutine event. Being nonroutine, a project requires some planning. How much planning you need depends on the complexity of the project. The more complex the project or the more uncertain it is, the more you have to plan.

For example, if on a regular basis your job is to train employees to use a spreadsheet, for you the process requires little project management because the activities are familiar to you. On the other hand, it would be a significant project to coordinate training for several departments or to develop a new course.

The steps required to complete a project are called *tasks*. They are performed in a sequence determined by the nature of the project. Some tasks occur sequentially, one immediately after another, while other tasks occur simultaneously. The amount of time it takes to complete a task is its *duration*.

To get a task done you need *resources,* which can be people, supplies, equipment, or facilities. Because resources are seldom available 24 hours a day, seven days a week, you need to consider the *calendars* that specify their availability.

A project is the combination of tasks and resources directed toward accomplishing a specific goal.

Why Use a Computer to Plan a Project?

With Microsoft Project on your personal computer it is easy to create and modify a set of tasks to meet your goal. Use Microsoft Project to:

- Create a realistic project plan.

- Respond to changes quickly and realistically.

- Anticipate the unexpected and assess the consequences.

Project management software is an invaluable tool for establishing an initial project plan. In addition, Microsoft Project quickly recalculates schedules and lets you see how changes in part of the project affect your overall plan. New tasks, obsolete tasks, interim dates affecting other tasks, or the irregular availability of a resource might slip by unnoticed, but with Microsoft Project you can keep it all under control.

In addition, keeping everyone informed by presenting only the information they need could be a lot of work without the aid of a computer. Other resources need to know what they are expected to do and when they are supposed to do it. Your management needs to be kept informed about the progress of the project. With Microsoft Project you can quickly get the reports and information you need. You can also tailor reports and presentations to accommodate your special requirements.

Using Project Management Tools

Two basic tools help you get the answers you need throughout the project. The *Gantt Chart* tells you when tasks are scheduled. The *PERT Chart* helps you understand the relationship between tasks and why they are scheduled the way they are. As your information requirements change in the course of a project, the tool you use to get the information you want will also change.

The Gantt Chart

One of the most familiar tools for visualizing progress in a project is a Gantt Chart. As the following illustration shows, the Gantt Chart uses horizontal bars each representing a single task in the project.

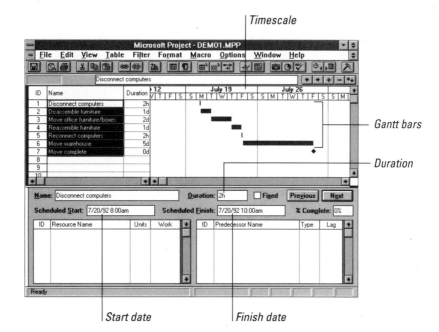

The bars are positioned across a period of time known as a *timescale*. The relative length of an individual Gantt bar represents the task's duration, the length of time it takes to complete a task. A basic fixture in project management, a Gantt Chart is an excellent tool for quickly assessing the status of individual tasks over time in a project.

The PERT Chart

When it is more important to know the relationships of the tasks in a project to one another, the PERT Chart (also known as the network chart) can be more illustrative than the Gantt Chart. As shown in the following illustration, the PERT Chart displays the interdependencies among tasks.

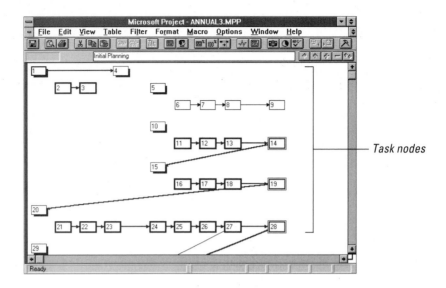

Task nodes

Each task is represented by a box, called a node, that contains basic information about the task. Tasks that depend on one another for completion or simply follow one another in a sequence of events are connected by lines. The PERT Chart gives you a graphical representation of how tasks are linked to each other in the project. In this book, detailed step-by-step exercises on using PERT Charts are in the Appendix.

Understanding Critical Tasks

The *Critical Path Method* (CPM) is the process for determining which tasks are *critical* (tasks that if delayed would directly affect the completion date of the project.) Critical tasks are said to be on the *critical path*. With the critical tasks identified, you can focus on the tasks that require the closest management. Knowing which tasks are critical also helps you assign priorities and assess the effect of changes on the project.

CPM is also used to schedule the start and finish dates for individual tasks by taking into account the relationships between tasks, their duration, and any constraints regarding availability of resources. Microsoft Project uses CPM to schedule tasks in a project.

Setting Project Goals

When you are about to begin a project, start your preparations by determining *What is the goal of the project?* Be as specific as you can. In the following table are some examples of how general goals can be made more specific to facilitate better planning.

Too general	Better
Move company to new location.	Move office and warehouse to new location by December 15.
Write Annual Report.	Write and distribute Annual Report one month prior to shareholders meeting, scheduled for September 22.
Install and use new financial reporting system by year end.	Convert finance department and company department heads to new financial reporting system by second quarter for pilot phase. Convert entire organization by year end.

Notice that the more specific goals clarify the scope, who is affected, and the time frame.

One Step Further

To review project management concepts and to begin getting acquainted with the capabilities of Microsoft Project, you can start the Microsoft Project online Tutorial. There are 17 lessons in the Tutorial, which roughly correspond with the topics covered in the lessons in this book. You can run the Tutorial to review the topics in the previous lesson, or you can run the Tutorial lesson for the next topic to get a preview of the next lesson.

1   In Program Manager, double-click the Microsoft Project icon.

    This starts the Microsoft Project program.

2   From the Help menu, choose Tutorial.

3   Follow the instructions on the screen to select the lesson called "What is Project Management?" in the "Project Management Basics" section.

    When you have completed the lesson, you can go on to Lesson 2 in this book, "What is Microsoft Project?"

If You Want to Quit Microsoft Project for Now

1   From the File menu, choose Exit.

2   Choose the No button if you see a message box asking whether you want to save your work.

Lesson Summary

Project management means answering the following questions about a project:

- What, generally, needs to be done?
- What steps are needed to accomplish the goal?
- When does each step start?

- When does each step finish?
- Who or what is needed to perform each step?
- How much will it cost?
- What adjustments can be made to achieve the plan?
- How can project progress be presented to inform others?

With project management software like Microsoft Project, you can get the answers to these questions and still have time to do your job.

For More Information

The Tutorial is an excellent resource for getting an overview of project management principals in general and for learning to use Microsoft Project in particular. Another place to get an overview of project planning and the capabilities of the program is in the *Microsoft Project Feature Guide,* which accompanies your software.

Preview of the Next Lesson

In Lesson 2, you will learn about the Microsoft Project environment and the general steps for using the program to perform basic project management activities.

Learning Microsoft Project Basics

In this lesson, you'll get acquainted with the basics of using Microsoft Project. After you open and rename a sample project file, you'll see how Microsoft Project uses views to present the same project information in different ways. After moving around in the views and selecting project information, you'll use the entry bar to enter information into the project. Finally, you'll learn how to specify a start date to have Microsoft Project schedule the project for you.

You will learn how to:

- Open and close a project file.

- Save a project file with a new name.

- Change the active view and move around within a view.

- Select information in the project.

- Use the entry bar to enter information.

- Use the Project Information dialog box to schedule a project.

Estimated lesson time: 35 minutes

Start Microsoft Project

If you quit Microsoft Project at the end of "Getting Ready," or if you are beginning with this lesson, start Microsoft Project now.

▶ Double-click the Microsoft Project icon.

For information about starting Microsoft Project, see "Starting Microsoft Project" in the "Getting Ready" section earlier in this book.

The Task Entry view appears, ready for you to enter data. This view appears whenever you start a new project. You'll learn more about the Task Entry view in this lesson.

Opening a Project File

To begin, open a project file to use in this lesson.

The Open command   With the Open command on the File menu, you open a project file from a disk and display it in the Microsoft Project window.

Changing the current directory   You can use the File Open dialog box to change the current directory or drive. To change the current directory, select a directory from the Directories box and then choose the OK button, or double-click the directory name.

To change the current disk drive, select a drive from the Drive box and then choose the OK button, or double-click the drive designation.

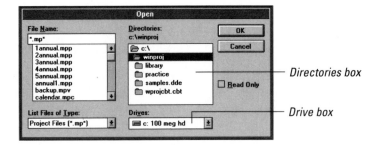

Directories box

Drive box

Open a project file

Do the following to open the project file called PRACT02.MPP.

1   From the File menu, choose Open.

2   In the Directories box, double-click the PRACTICE directory.

3   In the File Name box, select PRACT02.MPP.

4   Choose the OK button.

5   After the file is opened, press ALT+HOME to move the timescale to the beginning of the project.

Saving a Project File

It's a good idea to save your work any time you have made important changes to the project.

To store your work and changes in a project file, you have two options. From the Edit menu, you can use the Save command to save your changes. Using the Save button on the tool bar is the same as using the Save command from the File menu.

Save button

You can use the Save As command (also on the File menu) to rename a project file or change its location. When you use the Save As command, Microsoft Project closes the original file, and the project file with the new name becomes the current file.

Rename the file

The project file you opened already contains some sample tasks. Before you make any changes to this project, save the project with a new name so that you, or someone else, can reuse the original files.

1   From the File menu, choose Save As.

2   In the File Name box, type **MOVE02.MPP**

The period and extension (".MPP") are optional; they are added automatically if you don't type them.

3   Choose the OK button.

Microsoft Project stores your project on your hard disk with the filename MOVE02.MPP.

Displaying Project Information in Views

A *view* is a presentation format that you can use to enter and display project information. The default view (the view you see when you first open Microsoft Project) is called the *Task Entry view*. It contains a Gantt Chart in the top part of the window and the Task Form in the bottom part. The Gantt Chart includes a table on the left for quick entry of basic task information and a bar chart on the right. The Task Form displays additional information about whatever task is currently selected in the top view.

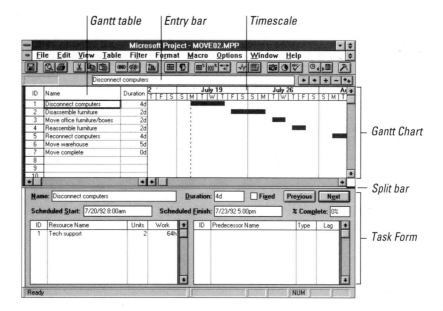

Displaying Single-Pane Views

Your screen is divided into two parts, with one view displayed in the top half of the screen and another in the bottom half. You can display a view to fill the entire screen by pressing SHIFT when you select the view from the View menu.

Display a single-pane Gantt Chart

▶   Hold down the SHIFT key, and from the View menu, choose Gantt Chart.

The Gantt Chart fills the entire screen.

Return to double-pane view

▶ Double-click the split box at the bottom of the vertical scroll bar.

The Task Form appears in the bottom view.

Looking at Other Views

The Task Entry view is just one of many ways in which you can examine project information. These views fall into three general categories: *Sheet views, Chart and Graph views,* and *Form views.* Throughout this book you'll have opportunities to work with a variety of views and learn about the important features of each. For now, here is a brief introduction of the different kinds of views you can use in Microsoft Project.

Sheet views   Display task or resource information in a rows-and-columns format, as in a spreadsheet. You can use sheet views to enter task or resource information. Use a sheet view when you want to see a lot of information at one time. The following illustration shows a Resource Sheet.

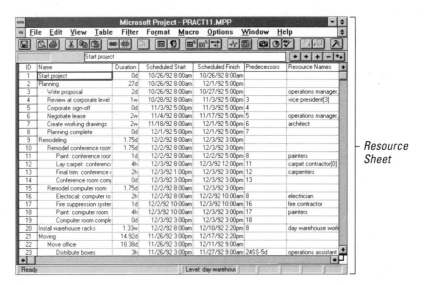

— Resource Sheet

Chart and Graph views   Provide graphical representations of project information. Use a charts or graph view when you need to present "the big picture" of the project plan to others. The following illustration shows a Resource Graph.

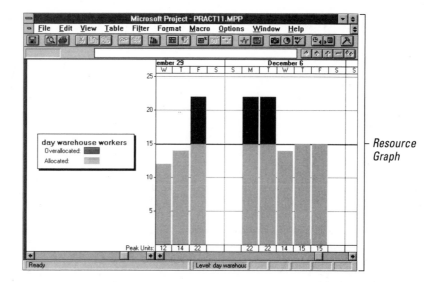

Resource Graph

Form views   Display task or resource information in a format similar to that which you complete with pencil and paper. Forms contain the same information you see in the sheet view, but help you focus on information about a specific task or resource. Use a form view when you want to examine task or resource information in detail. The following illustration shows a Resource Form.

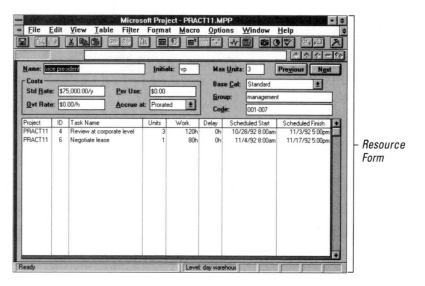

Resource Form

Combining Views

Combination views display two different types of views at the same time. The top of the screen contains one view, and the bottom contains another. These views are paired in combinations that are especially useful when you are dealing with specific project management operations. For example, the Task Entry view (the default view) is a combination view that contains a Gantt Chart in the top window and a Task Form in the bottom window. You use this view when you are entering task information. Like all combination views, the bottom part of the view displays detail information corresponding to the field selected in the top part.

Another useful combination view is the *Resource Allocation view*. This view is made up of the *Resource Usage view* in the top part and the *Delay Gantt Chart* in the bottom part. The Resource Allocation view is useful when you want to examine the tasks to which a specific resource is assigned. The Resource Allocation view looks like the following illustration.

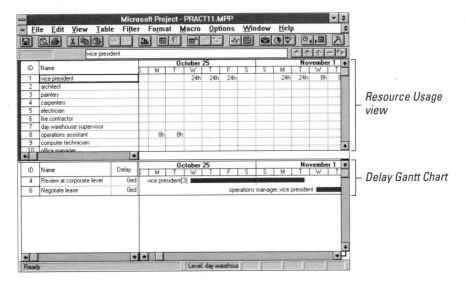

Resource Usage view

Delay Gantt Chart

Make your own combination view

Even though there are many views from which you can choose, you can make your own combination views to fit your specialized information requirements.

1   Click the top view.

2   From the View menu, choose Resource Sheet.

The Resource Sheet view displays all the resources in the project.

3   Click the bottom view.

4   From the View menu, choose Task Sheet.

The Task Sheet view displays the tasks to which a selected resource is assigned. Your combination view looks like the following illustration.

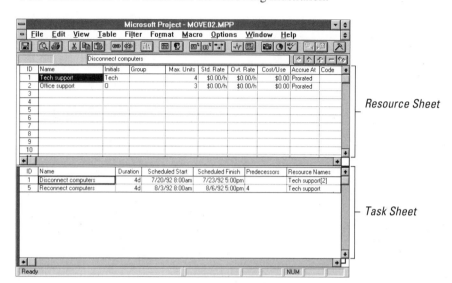

Resource Sheet

Task Sheet

5   In the Resource Sheet, select the first resource.

The Task Sheet displays the tasks to which the first resource is assigned.

6   In the Resource Sheet, select the second resource.

The Task Sheet displays the tasks to which the second resource is assigned.

7   From the View menu, choose Task Entry

Moving Around in a View

A view often contains more information than what is currently displayed on the screen. To see additional columns of task information, you can scroll through the Gantt table on the left. Scroll down through the list of tasks to see additional tasks. To see more of the timescale, you can use the horizontal scroll bar on the Gantt Chart. There are also keyboard shortcuts that let you move quickly around the Gantt view. When you move around in the Gantt table, the timescale on the Gantt Chart does not move. Similarly, when you scroll though the timescale on the Gantt Chart, the Gantt table does not move. However, if you scroll vertically in the view, both the Gantt Chart and the Gantt table move simultaneously.

You can also switch between the top and bottom views so that you can work in either view.

Moving in the Gantt Chart

In the Gantt Chart (on the right side of the top view), Microsoft Project represents the current date (according to the Current Date in the Project Info dialog box) with a dashed vertical line called the *date line*. The Gantt Chart displays the date line in the center of the Gantt Chart by default. Depending on the current date, the start of the project might not be visible.

When you scroll horizontally through the Gantt Chart, you are moving through the timescale. If you have more tasks than will fit in the view, you need to use the vertical scroll bar to see the tasks and their corresponding Gantt bars.

Scroll through the project with the mouse

1   Click the arrow at the right end of the horizontal scroll bar.

   Microsoft Project moves the timescale approximately one week further into the project.

2   Drag the scroll box to the middle of the horizontal scroll bar.

   The timescale moves further into the project.

Use a keyboard shortcut to move to the start of the project

▶   Press ALT+HOME to move the timescale to the start of the project.

Moving in the Gantt Table

You enter specific project information in *fields*. In forms, the name of the field appears next to the box where you enter information. In tables, where the fields are aligned in rows and columns, field names appear at the top of the column. A field is selected when it is surrounded by a bold, black border. You can use either the mouse or the keyboard to select fields in the Gantt table.

Use the mouse to select fields

▶   Click in the second row of the Name field in the Gantt table. This is the Name field for task 2.

   The Name field for task 2 is selected.

Use the keyboard to select fields

You can also use the keyboard to select the field where you want to work.

1   Press TAB to move to the Duration field.

2   Press TAB four more times to move to the Resource Names field.

   The Resource Names field is the last field in the Gantt table. Notice that the first fields scroll off to the left of the screen as new fields you select scroll on to the screen from the right.

3   Press SHIFT+TAB to move to the previous field, Predecessors.

4   Press the DOWN ARROW twice to move down two rows.

Scroll in the Gantt table

You can use the scroll bar to see different parts of the table without selecting any field.

1   Click the left arrow at the left end of the horizontal scroll bar.

Notice that the last field scrolls off the right edge of the table and a new field scrolls on from the left in small increments.

2   Click to the right of the scroll box in the horizontal scroll bar.

Notice that more new fields scroll from the right as fields scroll off the left in larger increments.

3   Drag the scroll box all the way to the left edge of the horizontal scroll bar.

The Name field appears as the first field in the table, but it is not selected. Moving around with the scroll bar does not change the selected cell.

Use a keyboard shortcut to select the first field in the project

▶   Press CTRL+HOME to select the first field in the first row.

Select an entire row

▶   Click a number in the ID field.

All the information for this task is selected (even that which is not visible in the table).

Using the Entry Bar

You can use the *entry bar* to enter and edit text in specific fields. When you click in a field—either in a sheet view or in the table part of a form view—the contents of the field appears in the entry bar. When you click in the entry area, the enter box (the check mark) and the cancel box (the "X") appear next to the entry area. Click the enter box when you complete an entry. Click the cancel box to retain the original entry.

When you click in a field that contains a list of options from which you can choose, an arrow appears in the entry bar. You use the arrow in the entry bar to see a list of valid entries for that field. Making a selection from the entry bar is often faster than typing an entry in a field.

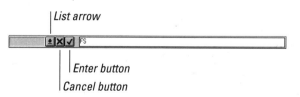

List arrow

Enter button

Cancel button

Change the active view

▶   Click the Task Form in the bottom view.

Now the bottom view is active.

Display an entry bar list

1   Click inside the Type field in the table at the lower right.

2   Click the arrow in the entry bar.

The entry bar list displays a list of relationship types.

3   Press ESC to clear the drop-down list.

4   Click inside the Resource Name field in the lower-left table.

5   Click the arrow in the entry bar.

The entry bar list displays a list of resources.

Change the active view

▶   Click the Gantt table in the top view.

Now the top view is active.

Select a field

▶   Click the first row of the Duration field.

The entry area contains the entry "4d."

Enter text in a field

1   Click the first blank row in the Name field.

The entry area is empty.

2   Type **Order food for moving party.**

The entry area contains the text you type.

Enter box

3   Choose the enter box on the entry bar to place the text in the field.

The enter box is the check mark next to the entry area.

Working with Menus

Moving between views changes the commands available in some menus. For example, when you select the Format menu from the Task Form, it contains a different list of commands than when you select Format from the Gantt table.

Change the active view

▶ Click the Task Form in the bottom view.

Now the bottom view is active.

Open the Format menu

▶ Click Format in the menu bar.

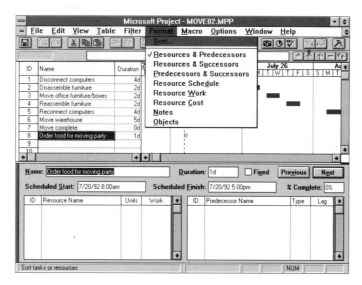

The list of commands looks like the following illustration.

Change the active view

▶ Click the Gantt table in the top view.

Now the top view is active.

Open the Format menu

▶ Click Format in the menu bar.

The Format menu now contains commands different from the ones available when you were in the Task Form view. The list of commands looks like the following illustration.

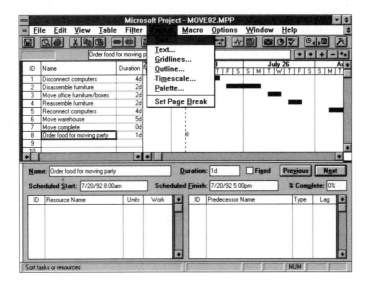

Displaying Dialog Boxes

Double-clicking in certain fields and in some parts of a view can display dialog boxes that let you make changes to the element you selected. For example, when you double-click in a field containing task information, you can display the Task Edit Form dialog box. When you double-click on the timescale in the Gantt Chart, you see the Timescale dialog box. Although you can open dialog boxes by choosing commands from a menu, double-clicking offers an excellent shortcut.

Open and close the Task Edit Form dialog box

1   In the Gantt table, double-click the Name field for task 1, "Disconnect computers."

Microsoft Project displays the Task Edit Form.

2   Choose the Cancel button to close the dialog box.

Open and close the Palette dialog box

1   Double-click anywhere within the Gantt Chart.

Microsoft Project displays the Palette dialog box.

2   Choose the Cancel button to close the dialog box.

Scheduling a Project

The Project Information dialog box is where you enter the project start date or finish date to do basic project scheduling. If you do not enter a project start or finish date, Microsoft Project starts your project on the day to which your computer's system clock is set.

Enter project information

You can get a quick overview of a project with the Project Information dialog box. In the following steps you enter the project name, the company name, and your name as project manager. You can choose to have this general project information appear when you print reports.

1   From the Options menu, choose Project Info.

The Project Information dialog box appears with the blinking insertion point in the Project box, ready for you to type the project name.

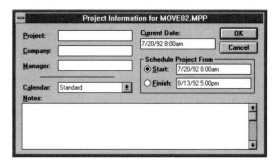

2   In the Project box, type **Victory Sports Move** to name the project.

If you make a typing mistake, press BACKSPACE to remove the error.

3   Press TAB to move to the Company box.

4   Type **Victory Sports**

5   Press TAB to move to the Manager box.

6   Type your name in this box.

Set a start date

Unless you specify a start date in the Project Info dialog box, your project is scheduled to begin on the current date. When you enter the project start date, Microsoft Project will compute a project finish date based on information entered in the project file.

When the project was first started, the kickoff date was July 20, 1992. Like many projects, activities were delayed. The Victory Sports move is now scheduled to begin October 26, 1992. Enter the new start date.

1   Under Schedule Project From, select the Start box.

2   Type **10/26/92**

Although you can enter the exact time of day you want a project to begin, by default Microsoft Project schedules the project to begin at 8:00 A.M. on the date you specify.

3   Choose the OK button.

Microsoft Project recalculates the schedule, based on the new start date.

Move to the start of the project

▶   Press ALT+END to move the timescale to the end of the project.

The new finish date is November 19, 1992.

Save button

Save your project

▶   Click the Save button on the tool bar.

One Step Further

Project notes are a great way to remind yourself to complete tasks or to leave information for others who may be working on the project. Work through these steps to enter a note to an assistant.

1   From the Options menu, choose Project Info.

2   In the Notes box, type **Payroll questions–call Pat. Keep Jim updated regarding schedule changes**.

If you make a typing mistake, press a direction key until the insertion point is just after the error. Press BACKSPACE. To start a new line, press SHIFT+ENTER.

3   Choose the OK button to confirm your entries.

4   Click the Save button on the tool bar.

If You Want to Continue to the Next Lesson

Save and close your project file

1   From the File menu, choose Close.

2   Choose the Yes button if you see the message box asking whether you want to save your work.

If You Want to Quit Microsoft Project for Now

Save and quit Microsoft Project

1   From the File menu, choose Exit.

2   Choose the Yes button if you see the message box asking whether you want to save your work.

Lesson Summary

To	Do this
Open a project file	Choose the Open command from the File menu. Then, from the File Name box, double-click on the name of the project you want to open.
Save a project file	Choose the Save command from the File menu. If this is the first time you are saving this file, enter the name you want for the file in the FileName box. You can also click the Save button on the tool bar to get the Save Dialog box.
Save and rename a file	Choose the Save As command from the File menu. Enter the name you want for the file in the File Name box.
Make a different field active	Click another field to select it.
Make another view active in a combination view	Click another view.
Enter text in a field	Select the field and begin typing.
Display fields in columns currently hidden in a table	Click the right arrow on the horizontal scroll bar.
Move the timescale to the start of the project	Press ALT+HOME.
Move the timescale to the end of the project	Press ALT+END.
Select the first field in the first task	Press CTRL+HOME.
Close a project file	Choose the Close command from the File menu.
Use online Help	Choose the Help command from the Help menu. Press F1 to get help from within a dialog box.
Schedule a project based on the earliest possible start date	Choose the Project Info command from the Options menu. Under Schedule Project From, enter the date you want the project to begin in the Finish box.

For more information, see in the *Microsoft Project User's Reference*

For an online lesson, see in the Microsoft Project for Windows Online Tutorial

Creating a Project—Entering Tasks

Preview of the Next Lesson

In the next lesson, you will learn to enter tasks in the task list and specify task durations. You'll also learn how to add, delete, move, and make changes to the task list.

Review & Practice

In the lessons in Part 1, "Learning the Basics," you learned skills to help you become familiar with planning a project. If you want to practice these skills and test your knowledge before you proceed with the lessons in Part 2, you can work through the Review & Practice section following this lesson.

Part 1   Review & Practice

Before you begin planning a project of your own, practice the skills you learned in Part 1 by working through the project management activities in this Review & Practice section. In the following practice exercise, you will open a practice project file and save it with a new name. Then you will use the Project Info command to schedule the project and enter general project information.

Scenario

The Review & Practice sections of this book are based on a realistic scenario in which Microsoft Project can help you do your job more effectively. Imagine that you are the communications manager at Victory Sports, Inc. This year you are responsible for leading the effort to produce and distribute the annual report. You will determine deadlines, assign people and departments to tasks, analyze costs, and communicate project progress. To help you in your role as project manager, you will enlist the aid of Microsoft Project to plan, coordinate, schedule, and report on the project.

You will review and practice how to:

- Open a project file.

- Specify a project start date to schedule a project.

- Complete the Project Information dialog box.

- Save a project.

Estimated practice time: 20 minutes

Step 1: Before You Begin...Plan!

After thinking about the goal of the project and the different major steps required to achieve the goal, your completed Project Plan Description form might look like the following illustration.

Project Name:
>   Victory Sports Annual Report

Project Goal:
>   To produce and distribute an annual report one week before Victory Sports' annual meeting, being held 9/22/92.

Project Phases:
>   Interview management
>   Assemble financial information
>   Develop text
>   Work with production team
>   Distribute reports

Project Milestones:
>   Final text is approved
>   Financial summaries are approved
>   Report goes to printer
>   Report packets sent

For more information on	See
Planning a project	Lesson 1

Step 2: Open a Project File

Open the scenario project file called 1ANNUAL.MPP. Before you make any changes in this project, save it with the new name ANNUAL1.MPP. Press ALT+HOME to scroll to the beginning of the project.

This project file contains tasks and milestones that correspond to the completed Project Plan Description form. Compare the task list in the project plan to the completed form above.

For more information on	See
Opening a file	Lesson 2
Saving a file	Lesson 2

Step 3: Enter Project Information

To open a dialog box in which you can enter general project information, choose the Project Info command from the Options menu.

Enter a start date

In the dialog box, under Schedule Project From, click the Start option button so that Microsoft Project schedules the project forward from start to finish. Enter 8/3/92 as the new start date.

Press ALT+HOME to move quickly to the new start date on the Gantt Chart.

Use the Project Plan Description form above to complete the remaining boxes in the Project Information dialog box. Enter the Project Goal in the Notes box.

For more information on	See
Entering a start date	Lesson 2

Save button

Save your project

▶ Click the Save button on the tool bar.

For more information on	See
Saving a project	Lesson 2

If You Want to Continue to the Next Lesson

Close your project file

▶ From the File menu, choose Close.

If You Want to Quit Microsoft Project for Now

Quit Microsoft Project

▶ From the File menu, choose Exit.

Part

2 Creating a Project

Entering Tasks in a Project

In this lesson, you will enter the tasks that comprise the framework of your project. After entering their duration, you will link them to establish the relationship between them, creating a schedule of events. You will also insert, move, and delete tasks to adjust for changing conditions in the project.

You will learn how to:

- Enter tasks and durations.
- Enter a milestone.
- Link tasks.
- Insert tasks.
- Move tasks.
- Delete a task.

Estimated lesson time: 45 minutes

Start Microsoft Project

If you quit Microsoft Project in the last lesson, you need to restart the application before you can continue.

▶ Double-click the Microsoft Project icon.

   If you need help starting Microsoft Project, see "Starting Microsoft Project" in the "Getting Ready" section earlier in this book.

Start the lesson

Do the following to open the project file called PRACT03A.MPP and rename it MOVE03A.MPP.

1 From the File menu, choose Open.

2 In the Directories box, double-click PRACTICE

   If necessary, scroll down the list to find it.

3 In the File Name box, double-click PRACT03A.MPP.

4 From the File menu, choose Save As.

5 In the File Name box, type **MOVE03A.MPP**

6 Choose the OK button.

Microsoft Project stores your project on your hard disk with the filename MOVE03A.MPP.

7 Press ALT+HOME to set the timescale at the beginning of the project.

This file is a version of the project you opened in Lesson 2. However, it contains no tasks—only the information for the project start date you entered with the Project Info command.

Working in the Task Entry View

The Task Entry view, which was introduced in Lesson 2, appears when you start a new project. The top part of the view is the Gantt Chart. It includes a table on the left side for quick entry of basic task information and a bar chart on the right. In the bar chart, Gantt bars are spread out over the timescale. Their length represents the length of a task. You can scroll through the timescale to see more of the schedule on the Gantt Chart. You can also scroll through the Gantt table on the left.

You can enter as much or as little task information as you like and watch your schedule take shape as you add each task.

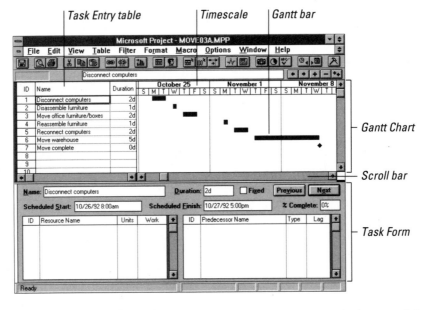

In Lesson 5 , you will learn how to complete the Task Form at the bottom of the screen to enter additional details about individual tasks.

Enter a task and duration

For the Victory Sports move, enter a list of the tasks that must occur after everything is packed. For example, before anything in the office can be moved, you need to disconnect the computers. You estimate this will take about two days.

1   Click the Name field for task 1.

2   Type **Disconnect computers**

If you make a typing mistake, press BACKSPACE.

Pressing TAB is an easy way to move from field to field.

3   Click the Duration field for task 1.

By moving to another field, the data you typed in step 2 is automatically stored in its field without your having to press ENTER.

The abbreviations for the duration units are:

w   weeks
d   days
h   hours
m   minutes

4   Type **2d** for a duration of two work days.

5   Click the Name field for task 2.

Note that a bar on the Gantt Chart now indicates a two-day duration, starting on Monday, October 26.

Your screen looks like the following illustration.

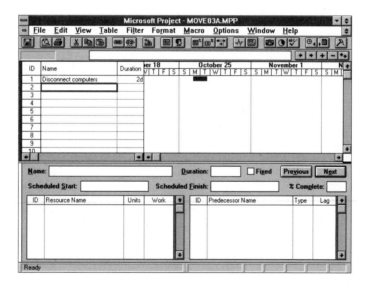

Save your project

It's a good idea to save your work any time you make important changes to the project.

Save button

▶ Click the Save button on the tool bar.

You can also choose the Save command from the File menu.

Adding Multiple Tasks

Although you can continue to enter each task and its duration individually, it is faster to enter several tasks and then go back and enter your estimates of the durations. When you enter a task, Microsoft Project automatically assigns a one-day duration (1d) as the default duration. First enter the following list of tasks, and then enter the durations.

Add several tasks

▶ Type the following tasks, pressing the DOWN ARROW key after each task.

You can also click the mouse in an empty Name field to enter another task.

```
Disassemble furniture
Move office furniture/boxes
Reassemble furniture
Reconnect computers
Move warehouse
```

The Gantt Chart looks like the following illustration.

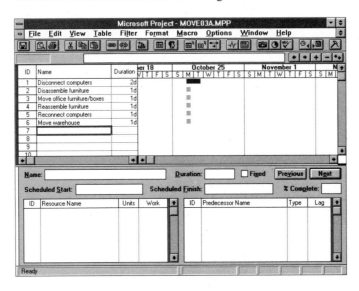

Add durations

Now that you have entered the tasks, go back and enter the duration of each task.

1   Click the Duration field for task 2 to select it.

2   Type the following durations; after each one, press the DOWN ARROW key to enter the duration and move to the next Duration field.

1d	*(task 2)*
2d	*(task 3)*
1d	*(task 4)*
2d	*(task 5)*
5d	*(task 6)*

Your Gantt Chart looks like the following illustration.

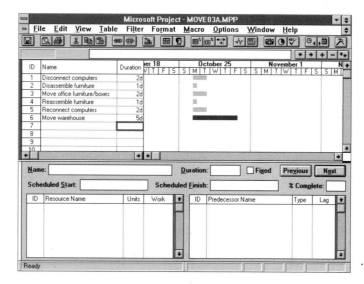

Enter a milestone

A *milestone* is a goal in your project. Entering a milestone is like entering a task, except that you type 0 (zero) for the duration. Use the next steps to enter a milestone called "Move complete."

1   Click the Name field for task 7 to select the field.

2   Type **Move complete**

3   Click the Duration field for task 7.

4   Type **0**

Enter box

5   Click the enter box on the entry bar.

Because the task has a duration of 0 (zero), the Gantt Chart shows the task as a diamond-shaped milestone.

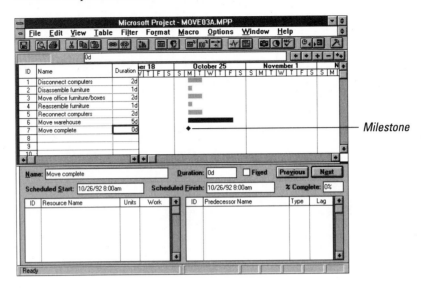

Milestone

Save button

Save your project

▶ Click the Save button on the tool bar.

Linking Tasks

Link Tasks button

A project is more than just a list of isolated tasks. Many tasks are related to each other. So far, although you've set up these tasks to follow one another in the task list, they all are scheduled to begin at the same time. This is because, even though you've assigned durations to the tasks, you have not yet told Microsoft Project when each task is to begin in relation to the other tasks. The quickest way to relate tasks is to *link* them with the Link Tasks button on the tool bar or the Link Tasks command on the Edit menu.

Linking tasks sets up a finish-to-start relationship between selected tasks. When one task finishes, the next task starts. In addition, linking tasks allows Microsoft Project to automatically calculate a schedule for your project. When you link tasks, Microsoft Project determines the start and finish dates for each task in the project. By linking tasks, you relate them to one another with the click of a button.

Selecting Tasks

First you select the tasks you want to link. You can select all of your tasks or select only a few. To select a group of contiguous tasks, click the first task and drag until you've selected the last task you want.

A quick way to select all the tasks in the project is to press CTRL+SHIFT+END after you select the first task.

To select a noncontiguous set of tasks, click the first task you want to select, and then hold down CTRL and click each individual task you want to add.

Select all the tasks

First, select the tasks you want to link.

▶   Click and drag the mouse from task 1 through task 7 in the Task Entry table.

Link the tasks

Link Tasks button

▶   Click the Link Tasks button on the tool bar.

You can also choose the Link Tasks command from the Edit menu.

Project links the tasks so that when one task finishes, the next task starts. A finish-to-start relationship is the most common type of relationship. In Lesson 5, you learn how to establish different kinds of relationships for tasks in a project.

Now that you've established task relationships, the bars on the Gantt Chart display the sequence of events. The length of each bar represents the duration of the task. The Gantt bar for the next task begins when the Gantt bar for the previous task ends.

Unlink Tasks button

Note   You can *unlink* selected tasks by clicking the Unlink Tasks button on the tool bar or by holding down SHIFT as you select the Edit menu and then choose the Unlink Tasks command.

The Gantt Chart with linked tasks looks like the following illustration.

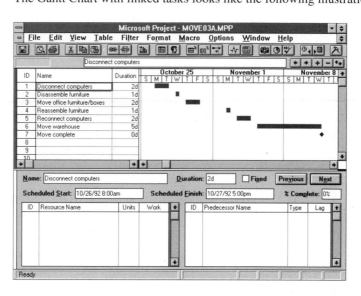

Save and close your project file

1   From the File menu, choose Close.

2   Choose the Yes button if you see the message box asking if you want to save your work.

Open a new file

Open a new version of the project. The new file contains additional tasks that you can edit.

1   From the File menu, choose Open.

2   In the Directories box, double-click PRACTICE.

3   In the File Name box, double-click PRACT03B.MPP.

4   From the File menu, choose Save As.

5   In the File Name box, type **MOVE03B.MPP**

6   Choose the OK button.

Microsoft Project stores a copy of your project on your hard disk with the filename MOVE03B.MPP.

7   Press ALT+HOME to set the timescale at the beginning of the project.

Editing the Task List

Microsoft Project makes it easy to plan and schedule tasks in a project. In addition, you can quickly add, move, and delete tasks as the details of the project change. With the following commands on the Edit menu, you quickly modify the task list.

Choose this command	To do this
Cut	Remove the selected information from the project and store it in a temporary holding area called the Clipboard. (See the "Getting Ready" section earlier in this book for more information about using the Clipboard.)
Copy	Copy the selected information onto the Clipboard, leaving the original information intact.
Paste	Insert the information currently on the Clipboard into the project. The Clipboard holds the most recently cut or copied information so you can paste it in as many places as you need.

The Cut, Copy, and Paste buttons on the tool bar are equivalent to the Cut, Copy, and Paste commands on the Edit menu. To cut or copy a task, you must select the entire row. This is easily done by clicking the ID number of the task you want to select.

From the Edit menu	On the tool bar
Cut	 *Cut button*
Copy	*Copy button*
Paste	*Paste button*

If you want to undo an editing change, select the Undo command on the Edit menu immediately after making the change. The Undo feature reverses only the most recent change.

Edit an entry

It's easy to change information you have entered. For example, "New site improvements" is more concisely described as "Remodeling."

1   Select "New site improvements."

2   Type **Remodeling**

3   Press ENTER.

You can also press the enter box on the entry bar. Your typing replaces the original entry.

Enter box

Insert a task

After you find a good site for Victory Sports' new location, you need to sell the idea to the corporate office. The next task is to write a proposal. You estimate you can complete it in two days. Before you can enter this task under "Locate a new site," you need to insert a blank row.

To insert a blank row, first select the row above which you want the new row to appear. The Insert command on the Edit menu moves rows down to create a blank row and inserts the new row above the one you selected.

1   Select "Get permits."

2   From the Edit menu, choose Insert.

Microsoft Project inserts a blank row. "Get permits" and all the tasks below it move down to make room. Note that the task ID numbers are adjusted accordingly.

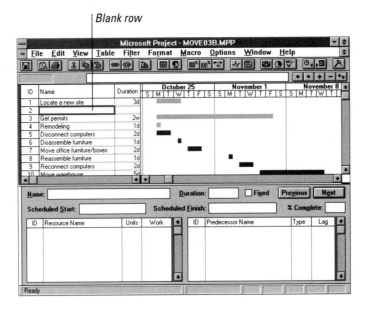

3   Type the following task and duration:

```
Write proposal 2d
```

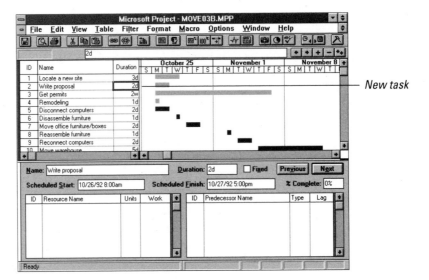

Move a task

When you move tasks from one location to the next, Microsoft Project automatically makes room at the new location; you don't need to insert blank rows when moving tasks.

Move "Get permits" from its current location to the row below "Remodeling" by cutting the task from its current location, and pasting it in a new location.

1 Click ID number 3 in the leftmost column to select the entire row for the "Get permits" task.

Cut button

2 Click the Cut button on the tool bar.

The task is removed from the task list and held in memory on the Clipboard. Other tasks move up.

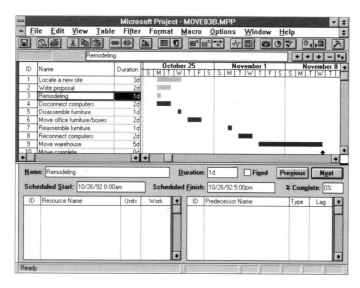

3 Select "Disconnect computers" (if it is not already selected) as the row above which you want "Get permits" to appear.

Paste button

4 Click the Paste button on the tool bar.

"Get permits" appears in the selected row. "Disconnect computers" and all the tasks that follow it are moved down on the task list. Task ID numbers reflect the change.

Moved task

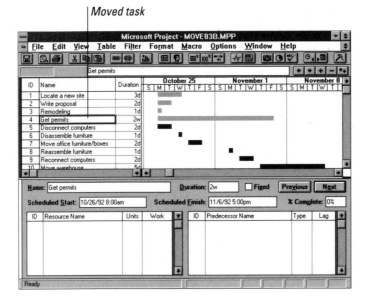

Save button

Save your project

▶ Click the Save button on the tool bar.

Delete a task

In your moving project, you realize that if you hire remodeling contractors, they can take care of the permits. You probably don't need to include the "Get permits" task in your project. Use the following steps to delete the task.

1   Select the "Get Permits" task, if it is not already selected.

When you add, move, or delete information, Microsoft Project adjusts the task ID numbers to reflect the change.

2   From the Edit menu, choose Delete.

You don't have to select the entire row to delete a task.

Microsoft Project removes the task from the task list.

Undo the deletion

On the other hand, maybe "Get permits" should stay in the task list until you make sure the contractors can take care of it. Microsoft Project gives you the opportunity to undo most commands. The Undo command reverses only the most recent operation.

▶ From the Edit menu, choose Undo Delete.

"Get permits" is restored to the task list.

If you change your mind about a command, the Undo command cancels your last editing command.

Link new tasks

The new tasks are all scheduled to start on the first day of the project. Because each of these tasks actually cannot start until the one before it is finished, you must link the new tasks to each other and to the "Disconnect computers" task.

1   Click and drag from tasks 1 through 5.

2   Click the Link Tasks button on the tool bar.

Link Tasks button

Microsoft Project reschedules the tasks so each task finishes before the next task begins in a finish-to-start relationship. In Lesson 5 you learn about other kinds of relationships you can specify for the tasks in your project.

Save your project

Save button

▶   Click the Save button on the tool bar.

One Step Further

Some tasks in the Scheduled Finish column might contain number signs (##). The signs indicate that the column is not wide enough to display the values in the column. This might vary depending on the display resolution you are using.

Another way to enter and examine task and scheduling information is through a spreadsheet-like table. The Task Sheet is a tabular view with many fields similar to the Task Entry view fields.

1   Move to the Gantt Chart.

2   From the View menu, choose Task Sheet.

3   Use the mouse or the arrow keys to move around the Task Sheet.

Entering data is identical to what you have been doing—simply select a field (for example, Name) and enter a task.

4   Double-click the "Scheduled Finish" heading.

5   Choose the Best Fit button.

The column expands so that you can now see the dates for the tasks.

6   From the View menu, choose Gantt Chart to prepare for the next lesson.

If You Want to Continue to the Next Lesson

Save and close your project file

1   From the File menu, choose Close.

2   Choose the Yes button if you see the message box asking whether you want to save your work.

If You Want to Quit Microsoft Project for Now

Save and quit Microsoft Project

1   From the File menu, choose Exit.

2   Choose the Yes button if you see the message box asking whether you want to save your work.

Lesson Summary

To	Do This
Enter a task	Click in a Name field and type the description of the task; then click the enter box on the entry bar or press ENTER.
Enter a duration	Click in the Duration field and type the duration of the task; then click the enter box on the entry bar or press ENTER.
Enter a milestone	Click in the Duration field and type 0 (zero) for the duration of the task; then click the enter box on the entry bar or press ENTER.
Link tasks	Select the tasks and click the Link Tasks button on the tool bar.
Insert a task	Select the row above which you want a task inserted; use the Insert command on the Edit menu to insert a blank row. Enter task information in the new row.
Move a task	Cut the selected task with the Cut button. Select a row in the new location; then use the Paste button to place your selection.
Delete a task	Choose the Delete command from the Edit menu to delete a selected task.
Undo a command	Choose the Undo command from the Edit menu to reverse an action.

For more information, see in the *Microsoft Project User's Reference*

For more information, see in the *Microsoft Project User's Reference*

For an online lesson, see in the Microsoft Project for Windows Online Tutorial

Preview of the Next Lesson

Now that you are familiar with the basics of entering tasks and durations, you are ready to discover how outlining can add structure to your task list. By arranging tasks in a hierarchical structure, as in the next lesson, you will see how the detail tasks fit within broader task categories.

Outlining Your Project

You can have up to 10 levels of subordinate tasks under a summary task.

In this lesson, you'll learn how to outline your project tasks. Outlining is a method of organizing tasks so you can see the structure of your project. You can arrange tasks in a hierarchical structure that helps you see how detail, or *subordinate*, tasks fit within broader categories, or *summary tasks*. With outlining, you also have the ability to collapse and expand the outline to present project information easily with just the right level of detail.

You will iearn how to:

- Create a summary task.
- Demote tasks.
- Collapse and expand the outline.
- Edit outline and summary tasks.
- Collapse and expand summary tasks.

Estimated lesson time: 40 minutes

Start Microsoft Project

If you closed Microsoft Project in the last lesson, you need to restart the application before you can continue.

▶ Double-click the Microsoft Project icon.

Start the lesson

Do the following to open the project file called PRACT04.MPP and rename it MOVE04.MPP.

1   From the File menu, choose Open.

2   In the Directories box, double-click PRACTICE.

3   In the File Name box, double-click on PRACT04.MPP.

4   From the File menu, choose Save As.

5   In the File Name box, type **MOVE04.MPP**

6   Choose the OK button.

Microsoft Project stores your project on your hard disk with the filename MOVE04.MPP.

7   Press ALT+HOME to move the Gantt Chart to the start of the project.

The new project contains three new tasks: "Planning," "Moving," and "Move Office." They have been entered near related tasks to illustrate how to use outlining in this lesson.

Understanding Summary Tasks

Summary tasks are general headings with subordinate tasks indented below them. Summary tasks provide an outline structure that identifies the project's major phases. As in any outline, each level of indenting represents an additional level of detail for the task. You create a summary task when you indent (or *demote*) the task below it. You remove the outline structure when you *promote* detail tasks below a summary task.

A summary task is automatically scheduled to start on the earliest start date of its earliest subordinate tasks; its finish date is the latest finish date of its last subordinate tasks. A summary task's duration is the total working time between the earliest start and latest finish dates of its subordinate tasks.

Summary tasks also contain total work and cost information.

Changing the Outline by Demoting and Collapsing Tasks

You can *collapse* the outline to show only the summary tasks and hide the more detailed tasks. You can also *expand* summary tasks so that all the subordinate tasks are revealed in the plan. By collapsing and expanding specific summary tasks or all the summary tasks in the project, you have the ability to view and print the amount of detail that you need.

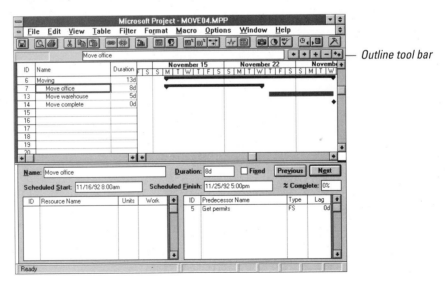

— Outline tool bar

With the mouse, you can click an outline button to promote, demote, collapse, expand individual tasks, or expand all tasks. The outline buttons are located on the outline tool bar near the top right edge of the screen. You can also use the keyboard to promote and demote tasks and to collapse and expand the outline.

Outline button	Function
	Demote a task to a lower level
	Promote a task to a higher level
	Expand a task to view its subordinate tasks
	Collapse a task to hide its subordinate tasks
	Expand all tasks to view all subordinate tasks

Demoting tasks

Demoting tasks is how you establish an outline structure for your project. The task immediately above the first task you demote becomes a summary task.

Five of the tasks you entered earlier, from "Disconnect computers" through "Reconnect computers," are all part of moving the office. Demote these five tasks so they are indented under "Move office."

Demote several tasks

1   Select tasks 8 through 12.

2   Click the Demote button on the outline tool bar.

3   If necessary, scroll the Gantt Chart to view the new summary bar.

Demote button

The selected tasks become subordinate tasks. "Move office" is now a summary task because it has subordinate tasks—tasks demoted under it. The duration of "Move office" changes to summarize the duration of the five subordinate tasks. Since the earliest task starts at 8:00 a.m. on November 16, and the latest task finishes at 12:00 P.M. on November 25, the duration is 8d. Scroll the Gantt Chart to the week of November 15.

Your Gantt Chart looks like the following illustration.

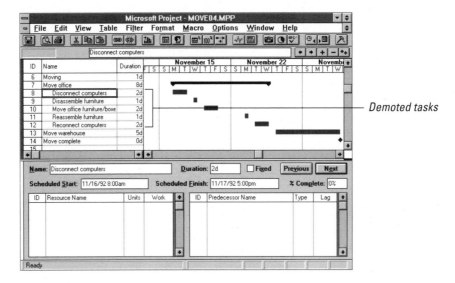

Demoted tasks

4 Select all rows from "Move office" through "Move complete" to select tasks 7 through 14.

Demote button

5 Click the Demote button on the outline tool bar.

The "Move office," "Move warehouse," and "Move complete" tasks are demoted one level. The tasks you demoted earlier remain demoted under the "Move office" task so the outline form is maintained.

You've outlined the "Moving" phase of the project. It should look like the following illustration.

Task demoted one level

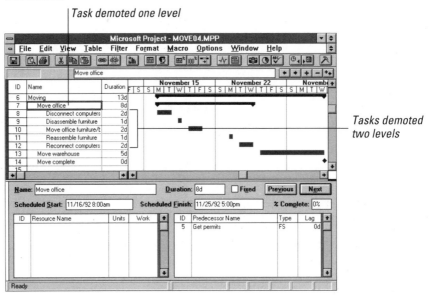

Tasks demoted two levels

Save button

Save your work

▶   Click the Save button on the tool bar.

Collapsing and Expanding Tasks

Not everyone interested in your project requires the same level of detail as you do. For example, the branch manager of Victory Sports has requested an overview of the project. To provide only the required information, you can collapse the "Move office" task. Collapsing a task means you can "hide" the subordinate tasks. When you collapse the summary tasks, you can display the level of detail appropriate for the branch manager's request.

Collapse a summary task

1   Select the "Move office" summary task.

Collapse button

2   Click the Collapse button on the outline tool bar.

All the tasks assigned to the "Move office" summary task are hidden.

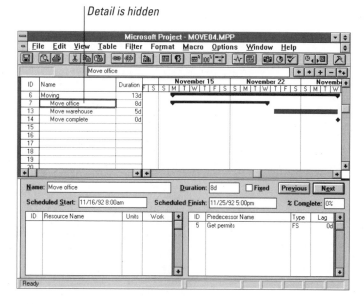

Collapse another summary task

Notice that "Moving" is also a summary task. Collapsing it will hide even more detail.

1   Select the summary task "Moving."

Collapse button

2   Click the Collapse button on the outline tool bar.

All the tasks assigned to "Moving" are hidden. The Gantt Chart displays the combined duration of the hidden tasks.

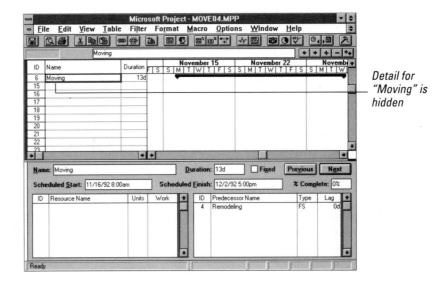

Detail for "Moving" is hidden

Display all tasks by expanding them

Even if you collapse the summary tasks one at a time, you can still expand them all at once.

Expand all button

▶ Click the Expand All button on the outline tool bar.

All detail tasks are revealed as shown in the following illustration.

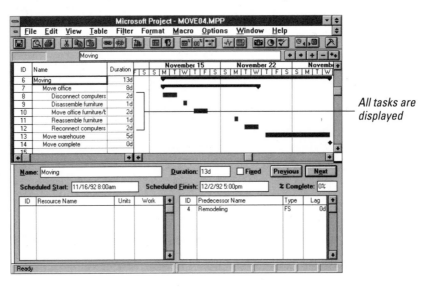

All tasks are displayed

Save button

Save your work

▶ Click the Save button on the tool bar.

Using Outline Numbers

As you demote tasks to form an outline, Microsoft Project assigns outline numbers to the tasks. The outline numbers indicate the levels of subordinate tasks. Any changes you make to the outline of the task list are automatically reflected in the outline numbers.

Use the Outline command on the Format menu to view outline numbers.

View the outline numbers

As you demoted tasks to show the steps involved in the "Moving" phase, Microsoft Project automatically assigned outline numbers to each task. This number is useful for sorting your tasks into related groups. Take a look at the assigned numbers using the Outline command.

1   From the Format menu, choose Outline.

2   Click the Outline Number check box to place an **X** in it.

3   Choose the OK button.

The outline numbers precede the task name to indicate the task's exact position in the outline. For example, the number 6.1 for "Move office" indicates that this is the first task subordinate to the sixth task in the project.

Your task list should look like the following illustration.

Outline numbers are displayed

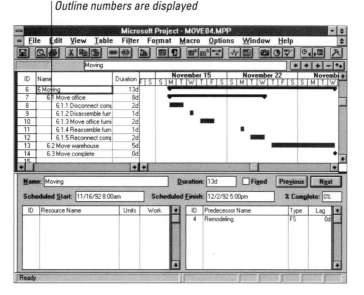

Turn off the outline numbers

To turn off the outline numbers, you clear the Outline Number check box.

1 From the Format menu, choose Outline.

2 Click the Outline Number check box to clear it.

When a check box is cleared, the X no longer appears in the box.

3 Choose the OK button.

Save button

Save your work

▶ Click the Save button on the tool bar.

Editing Summary Tasks

In an earlier lesson, you learned how to edit the task list by moving, deleting, and copying tasks. Although the procedures for editing summary tasks are similar, there are a few important differences. Summary tasks actually represent a set of subordinate tasks; therefore, when you edit a summary task, its subordinate tasks are also affected.

For example, if you delete a summary task, the tasks assigned to it are also deleted. Similarly, if you move a summary task, the subordinate tasks are also moved. If you do not want to affect the subordinates tasks, reassign them to another summary task.

Task ID numbers are automatically adjusted to reflect the changes to the summary and subordinate tasks.

Inserting and Linking New Tasks

In your moving project, you need to allow one week for the head office to review the proposal. The corporate sign-off that occurs after the review is the first milestone in the project. Once you've got the sign-off, you can get construction permits for the remodeling. As a result, you will need to insert tasks for the corporate review, getting the sign-off, and finally getting permits.

Insert several blank rows

It's easy to insert several rows at a time. First, select the first row above which you want to insert a blank row. Then select the number of rows that you want inserted. For example, if you want to insert two blank rows (as in the following steps), you select two rows, starting with "Remodeling." Microsoft Project inserts as many rows as you select above the starting row. Use the following steps to insert rows before inserting the tasks.

1 Select the Name field for task 4, the first row above which you want to insert a blank row.

2 Drag from task 4 through task 5.

3 From the Edit menu, choose Insert.

Two new, blank rows appear above the rows you selected.

Your task list should look like the following illustration.

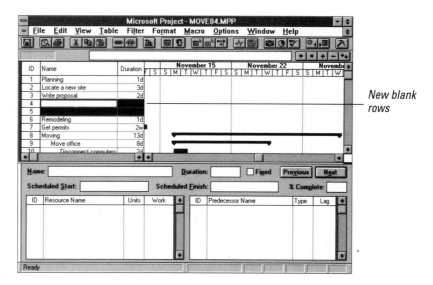

New blank rows

Insert new tasks

Now enter the two tasks and milestone in the new rows. To enter the milestone, be sure to type a 0 (zero) in the Duration field.

1 Click the Name field for task 4.

2 Enter the following tasks and durations for tasks 4 and 5.

```
Review at corporate level     1w
Corporate sign-off            0
```

Link new tasks

Link these tasks to indicate they will take place one after another.

1 Click in task 3, "Write proposal," and drag through task 6, "Remodeling."

2 Click the Link Tasks button on the tool bar.

3 Scroll the Gantt Chart to the week of October 25.

Your task list should look like the following illustration.

Link Tasks button

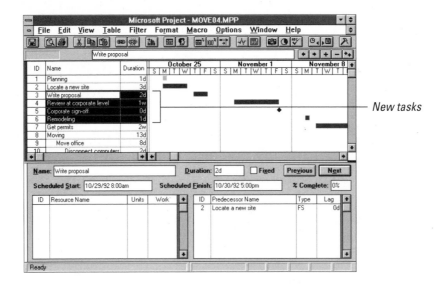

New tasks

Demote the tasks

The new tasks should also be demoted one level to show they are all part of "Planning" tasks.

1   Click in task 2 and drag through task 6.

2   Click the Demote button on the outline tool bar.

Demote button

"Planning" becomes a summary task. Its duration reflects the starting date of the first planning task, "Locate a new site," and the finish date of the last planning task, "Remodeling."

Your task list should look like the following illustration.

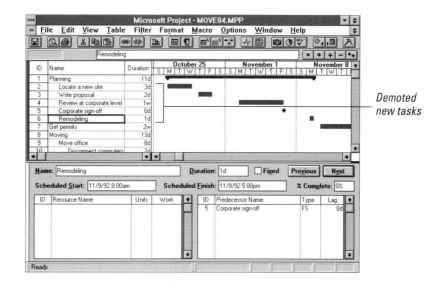

Demoted new tasks

Save button

Save your work

▶ Click the Save button on the tool bar.

Collapse and expand the outline

Collapse button

1   Select task 1 through task 16 to select all the tasks.

To quickly select all the tasks, click on task 1, and then press CTRL+SHIFT+END.

2   Click the Collapse button on the outline tool bar.

Your task list looks like the following illustration.

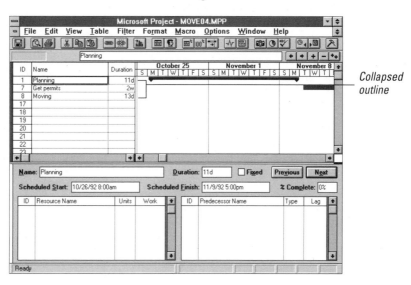

Collapsed outline

Expand All button

3   Click the Expand All button on the outline tool bar.

Your expanded outline looks like the following illustration.

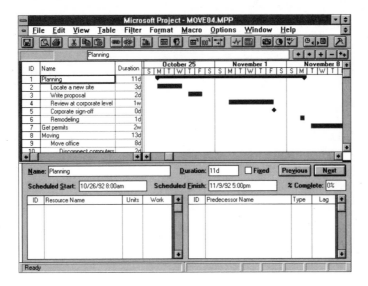

Save button

Save your work

▶ Click the Save button on the tool bar.

One Step Further

Earlier in this lesson, you applied an outline structure to detail and higher level tasks. This "bottom up" approach is useful if you plan to begin your project planning by brainstorming all tasks and later organizing them under summary tasks. An alternative to this approach, "top down" planning, is useful when you know what the general phases of the project are, and plan to fill in specific detail tasks later. In the following steps, you enter three new detail tasks under "Get permits." Then, demote them to make "Get permits" a summary task. Give tasks 8 and 9 a one-week duration each; make task 10 a milestone.

1   Insert three blank rows under "Get permits."

2   In the Name field for task 8, type the following new tasks and durations.

```
Complete application forms      1w

Submit requisitions for fees    1w

Submit applications       0
```

3   Select the three new tasks and link them.

4   While they are still selected, demote them to reflect that they are subordinate to the "Get permits" summary task.

If You Want to Continue to the Next Lesson

Save and close your project file

1   From the File menu, choose Close.

2   Choose the Yes button if you see the message box asking whether you want to save your work.

If You Want to Quit Microsoft Project for Now

Save and quit Microsoft Project

1   From the File menu, choose Exit.

2   Choose the Yes button if you see the message box asking whether you want to save your work.

Lesson Summary

To	Do this
Create a summary task	Select the task below the one that is going to be a summary task. Click the Demote button on the outline tool bar.
Demote tasks	Click the Demote button on the outline tool bar to demote selected tasks.
Collapse the outline	Click the Collapse button on the outline tool bar.
Expand the outline	Click the Expand All button on the outline tool bar.
Collapse summary tasks	Select summary tasks, then click the Collapse button on the outline tool bar.
Expand summary tasks	Click the Expand button on the outline tool bar to expand selected tasks.
Use outline numbers	From the Format menu, choose Outline; then click the Outline Number check box.

For more information, see in the *Microsoft Project User's Reference*

Copying Information   40

Deleting Information   93

Edit Commands   98

Editing Tasks and Resources   100

Moving Information   267

Outlining   296

For an online lesson, see in the Microsoft Project for Windows Online Tutorial

Outlining Tasks

Preview of the Next Lesson

In the next lesson, you'll learn how to schedule the sequence of tasks more precisely. You can use Microsoft Project to set up different task relationships, so that you can make the start or finish of one task depend on the start or finish of another task.

Establishing Task Relationships

In this lesson, you'll learn how to specify different types of relationships between the beginning and end points of related tasks. You'll also specify lead and lag times that represent the amount of overlap or time gaps between tasks.

You will learn how to:

- Specify finish-to-finish task relationships.
- Specify finish-to-start task relationships.
- Specify start-to-start task relationships.
- Specify lead and lag time task durations.

Estimated lesson time: 40 minutes

Start Microsoft Project

If you closed Microsoft Project in the last lesson, you need to restart the application before you can continue.

▶ Double-click the Microsoft Project icon.

Start the lesson

Do the following to open the project file called PRACT05.MPP and rename it MOVE05.MPP.

1   From the File menu, choose Open.

2   In the Directories box, double-click PRACTICE.

3   In the File Name box, double-click PRACT05.MPP.

4   From the File menu, choose Save As.

5   In the File Name box, type **MOVE05.MPP**

6   Choose the OK button.

   Microsoft Project stores your project on your hard disk with the filename MOVE05.MPP.

7   Press ALT+HOME to set the timescale at the beginning of the project.

Understanding Relationships Between Tasks

You can use Microsoft Project to set up task relationships, also known as *dependencies* or *precedence* relationships, so that you can make the start or finish of one task depend on the start or finish of another task. A task that must start or finish before another task can begin is called a *predecessor* task. A task that depends on the start or completion of another task is called a *successor* task.

In an earlier lesson, you learned how to use the Link Tasks command on the Edit menu to quickly establish finish-to-start relationships. Because there are other ways in which tasks can be dependent on one another, Microsoft Project also provides the ability to establish finish-to-finish, start-to-start, and start-to-finish relationships.

Updating the mailing list before printing the labels is an example of a finish-to-start relationship.

A *finish-to-finish* relationship is one in which both tasks finish at the same time. For example, you want your new computer to be completely installed and operational at the same time you have finished backing up the information on your old computer.

In a *start-to-start* relationship, two tasks start at the same time. For example, when building a house, you might arrange to start laying tile on both the bathroom floors and the kitchen countertops at the same time. Such a relationship could save time and money if your resources charge you for each trip to the site.

The *start-to-finish* relationship is less common than the others. But it can occur when the completion of one task depends on the start of a later task. For example, if an information systems department is converting to a new financial reporting system, the task "Run reports on old system" would not stop until "Run reports on new system" has started.

In addition, Microsoft Project allows you to include *lead* or *lag* (overlap or delay) time between tasks so you can accurately model real-world dependencies.

In this lesson, you insert a new task and then look for ways to tighten up the project schedule by modifying task relationships. First, go to the project finish date on the Gantt Chart. Then add one more task under the "Move office" summary task—distributing boxes to office employees so they can pack their own offices.

Add a task

1   Select task 13, "Disconnect computers," and insert a row.

2   In the Name field, type **Distribute boxes**

3   In the Duration field, type **3h**

4   Click the enter box on the entry bar or press ENTER.

    The new task assumes the outline level of the task below. You don't need to demote it.

Enter box

Your Task Entry view looks like the following illustration.

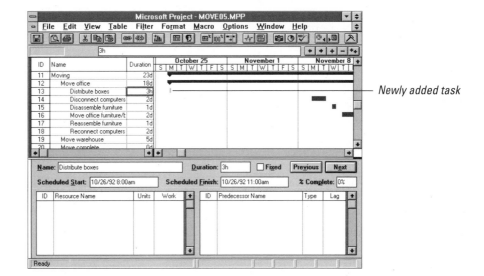

Newly added task

Save button

Save the project

▶ Click the Save button on the tool bar.

All tasks are still scheduled in finish-to-start relationships. "Disconnect computers," task 14, is still the successor to task 7, "Get permits." In the next steps, specify different relationships to tighten up the schedule.

Specifying Task Relationships

You can quickly set up predecessor and successor relationships between a series of tasks with the Link Tasks command on the Edit menu. When you choose this command or click the Link Tasks button on the tool bar, Microsoft Project sets up finish-to-start relationships between the selected tasks. Each task is linked to the previous task in the list so that one task can start as soon as the previous task is finished.

You may need to define different types of relationships between tasks other than finish-to-start. For example, you may want the start of a task to be dependent on the start of another task—a start-to-start relationship—or want the finish date of a task to depend on the completion of another task—a finish-to-finish relationship.

Entering Relationship Information

You can specify the task relationships on the Task Form, Gantt Chart, or Task Sheet. In this lesson you practice using all three methods.

As you move between the Gantt Chart and the Task Form, you can easily tell which view you're working in by looking at the bar on the left. The view in which you're working is called the *active view*.

Active view bar

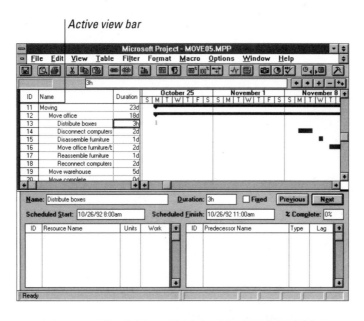

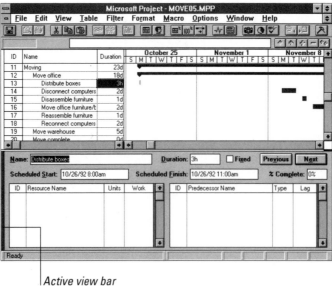

Active view bar

In the Predecessor field of the Task form, you can include the task ID number of the predecessor, lead or lag time, and the abbreviation for type of relationship: finish-to-start (FS), start-to-start (SS), finish-to-finish (FF), or start-to-finish (SF).

You can enter lead or lag time between tasks in minutes, hours, days, or weeks; elapsed minutes, hours, days, or weeks; or as a percentage of the duration of the predecessor task. For example, you can specify that a task start after half the duration of its predecessor. You can enter multiple predecessor relationships in the Predecessors field by separating each with a list separator character, such as a comma.

Enter a finish-to-finish relationship

The branch manager has asked you not to finish moving the office furniture until the warehouse move is completed. Use the Task Form to schedule a finish-to-finish relationship for these two tasks.

1   In the Gantt Chart, select task 19, "Move warehouse."

2   In the Task Form, click the number 18 in the predecessor ID column for "Reconnect computers."

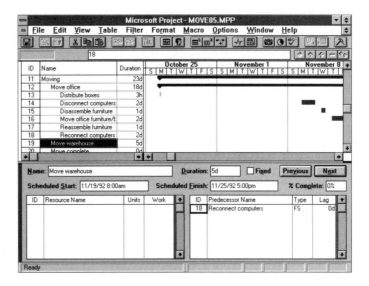

3   From the Edit menu, choose Delete to remove the predecessor.

4   In the ID column, type **16**

5   Click the Type column and type **FF**

FF stands for Finish-to-Finish.

6   Choose the OK button.

7   Click the Gantt Chart to make the top view active.

8 Scroll the timescale to the weeks of November 8 and November 15.

The Gantt bars for tasks 19 and 16 finish at the same time, displaying a finish-to-finish relationship, with both tasks finishing on November 13, 5:00pm.

Your Gantt Chart view looks like the following illustration.

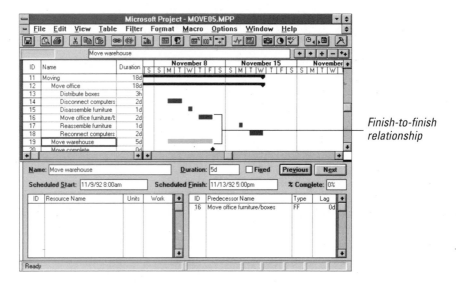

Finish-to-finish
relationship

Add a predecessor to "Move complete"

With this finish-to-finish relationship, you scheduled to finish moving items from the office and the warehouse at the same time. Next you need to add a predecessor to the "Move complete" milestone to indicate that the completion of the move is dependent on the finish of the last task under "Move office." Observe the location of the "Move complete" milestone as you complete these steps.

1 Select task 20, "Move complete."

2 In the Task Form, click just below the number 19 in the predecessor ID column.

3 Type **18**, the task ID number for "Reconnect computers."

4 Click the enter box on the entry bar or press ENTER.

5 Choose the OK button.

The "Move complete" milestone now occurs at the end of the "Move office" and "Move warehouse" tasks.

Your Gantt Chart view looks like the following illustration.

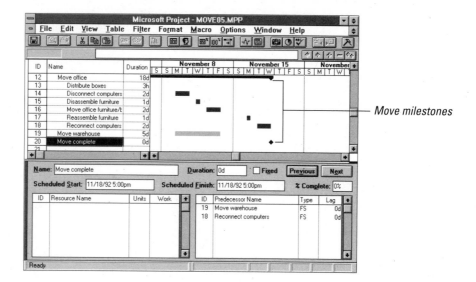

— Move milestones

Save button

Save the updated project

▶ Click the Save button on the tool bar.

Understanding Lead and Lag Time

In any type of task relationship, you can specify lead or lag time between tasks. In a finish-to-start relationship, an overlap between tasks is called lead time, where the start of the task precedes the finish of its predecessor. For example, you may want to start painting conference room walls when half of the computer room walls have been completed.

In a finish-to-start relationship, a gap or delay between two tasks is called lag time. For example, you may want to start laying carpet three days after painting is finished.

Specifying Lead Time

When you enter a lead time, you enter a minus sign (-) in front of the duration. For example, to specify a lead time of five days, you would enter **-5d**.

In the next exercise, you define a start-to-start relationship for the tasks "Distribute boxes" and "Disconnect computers." "Distribute boxes" needs five days of lead time. No matter when the office move is scheduled to start, you need to start distributing boxes five working days earlier.

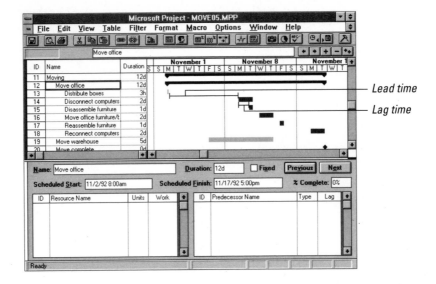

- Lead time
- Lag time

Enter start-to-start and lead time relationships

Make "Distribute boxes" the successor task to "Disconnect computers," so that it depends on when "Disconnect computers" starts. You can add lead time by changing the predecessor information for "Distribute boxes." This time you change a task relationship using the Gantt table.

1   Move to the Gantt table.

2   Click the right scroll arrow in the Gantt table to see the Predecessors column.

3   Select the Predecessors field of task 13, "Distribute boxes."

4   Type **14ss-5d**

"Disconnect computers" becomes the predecessor to "Distribute boxes" with a start-to-start relationship and 5 days of lead time.

5   Click the enter box on the entry bar or press ENTER.

The Predecessors field for task 13 reads "14SS-5d." Before specifying this relationship, "Distribute boxes" was scheduled to begin on October 26. Now with a start-to-start task relationship, with "Disconnect computers" and a 5-day lead time, "Distribute boxes" begins on November 2.

After completing these steps, your project will look like the following illustration.

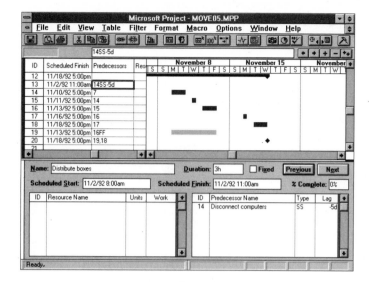

Specifying Lag Time

Lag time is the amount of overlapping between tasks. Currently all computers are scheduled to be disconnected before you start taking apart the furniture. You can save time by making these tasks overlap. In fact, you can start taking the furniture apart when 50 percent of the computers are disconnected. Since "Disconnect computers" is a two-day task, you can save a day by overlapping the tasks.

Use the next steps to schedule a start-to-start relationship with 50 percent lag time.

Enter percent lag time

1   Scroll the Gantt table so the Name column appears.

2   Select the successor task, "Disassemble furniture."

3   In the Task Form, click the Type field for the predecessor "Disconnect computers."

4   Type **ss**

5   Click the Lag field and type **50%**

    This indicates a start-to-start relationship with the second task starting after half of the first task is complete.

6   Click the enter box on the entry bar or press ENTER.

7   Choose the OK button.

    Now the tasks overlap, with "Disassemble furniture" starting one day after "Disconnect computers" begins. Your project will look like the following illustration.

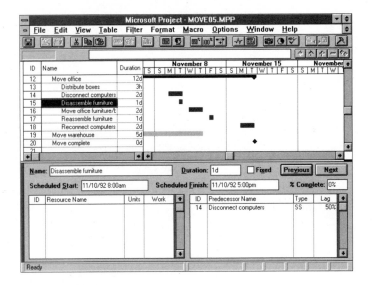

Save button

Save the updated project

▸ Click the Save button on the tool bar.

One Step Further

Microsoft Project has several features that make it easy to customize the display on your screen. Perhaps your company prefers certain symbols on the Gantt Chart, or you want critical tasks to be displayed in a particular color.

Change the shape and color of the milestone symbol, which is currently a black diamond. Before you continue, click anywhere in the Gantt Chart.

Double-clicking a blank area in the Gantt bar chart also displays the Palette dialog box.

1 From the Format menu, choose Palette.

2 In the Bar Name column, click the Milestone field to select it.

3 In the Shape box under Start, click the down arrow and use the scroll bar to display the list of shapes available.

4 Click the shape you want.

5 In the Color box under Start, click the down arrow to display the list of colors available.

6 Click the color you want.

7 Choose the OK button.

Experiment with other shapes if you like, but remember to return them to their original shape before you save this lesson so your work matches the screens in these lessons.

If You Want to Continue to the Next Lesson

Save and close your project file

1   From the File menu, choose Close.

2   Choose the Yes button if you see the message box asking whether you want to save your work.

If You Want to Quit Microsoft Project for Now

Save and quit Microsoft Project

1   From the File menu, choose Exit.

2   Choose the Yes button if you see the message box asking whether you want to save your work.

Lesson Summary

To	Do this
Specify a finish-to-finish task relationship	Enter FF in the Type field in the Predecessor section of the Task Form or Task Sheet.
Specify a finish-to-start task relationship	Enter FS in the Type field in the Predecessor section of the Task Form or Task Sheet.
Specify a start-to-start task relationship	Enter SS in the Type field in the Predecessor section of the Task Form or Task Sheet.
Specify a lead time task duration	Enter the duration of the lead time preceded by a minus sign (–) in the Lag field in the Predecessor section of the Task Form or following the type in the Predecessor field of the Task Sheet.
Specify a lag time task duration	Enter the duration of the lag time in the Lag field in the Predecessor section of the Task Form or following the type in the Predecessor field of the Task Sheet.

For more information, see in the *Microsoft Project User's Reference*

Lead and Lag Time   208

Task Relationships   535

For an online lesson, see in the Microsoft Project for Windows Online Tutorial

Assigning Task Relationships

Preview of the Next Lesson

Microsoft Project gives you control over the level of detail you see. Just as outlining and changing the units on the timescale changes the level of detail, you can filter project data to display or highlight only what you want to see. In the next lesson, you will work with filters to find tasks or resources that match the criteria you set.

Applying Project Filters

In this lesson, you'll learn to apply *filters*, which allow you to display or highlight only those tasks that match the criteria you select. You'll also create a custom filter to display information that is unique to your project. To make it easier to see the effects of this custom filter, you'll also learn how to adjust the timescale.

You will learn how to:

- Apply a filter to display information.
- Apply a filter to highlight information.
- Create a filter.

Estimated lesson time: 35 minutes

Start Microsoft Project

If you closed Microsoft Project in the last lesson, you need to restart the application before you can continue.

▶ Double-click the Microsoft Project icon.

Start the lesson

Do the following to open the project file called PRACT06.MPP and rename it MOVE06.MPP.

1 From the File menu choose Open

2 In the Directories box, double-click PRACTICE.

3 In the File Name box, double-click PRACT06.MPP.

4 From the File menu, choose Save As.

5 In the File Name box, type **MOVE06.MPP**

6 Choose the OK button.

   Microsoft Project stores your project on your hard disk with the filename MOVE06.MPP.

7 Press ALT+HOME to set the timescale at the beginning of the project.

Filtering Your Data Display

A *filter* contains a set of instructions, called *filter criteria*, that tells Microsoft Project which data to display or highlight when the filter is applied. There are two ways to apply filters. You can apply a filter so that only specific information is displayed; data that does not match is hidden. You can also apply a filter so that only the data that matches the filter criteria is highlighted; data that does not match is not highlighted.

Filters make it easier to manage large projects by displaying or highlighting only the information you need. For example, Microsoft Project supplies a Milestones filter that displays or highlights only milestone tasks. All other tasks are temporarily hidden or not highlighted. Remember that filters affect the screen display, but not the actual project.

Display the milestones

Your supervisor has requested a printout of the milestones in this project in order to stay on top of the move project. Milestones are scattered throughout the project, but Microsoft Project provides a filter that displays only the milestones. Be sure your timescale display is set at the start of the project, and then do the following.

▶ From the Filter menu, choose Milestones.

   The milestones are displayed, and all other task bars are hidden.

Your project looks like the following illustration.

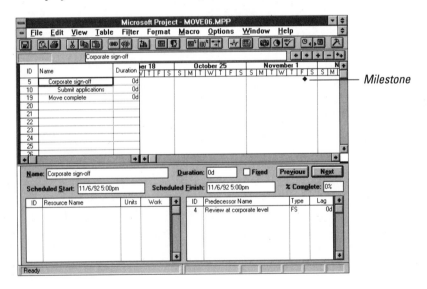

— Milestone

Highlight the milestones

You can display the Milestones filter as a highlighting filter instead.

Be sure to hold down the SHIFT key before selecting Filter from the menu.

▶ Hold down SHIFT as you choose Milestones from the Filter menu.

   All the tasks are displayed again, but the milestones are now highlighted in the table in blue or bold.

Your project looks like the following illustration.

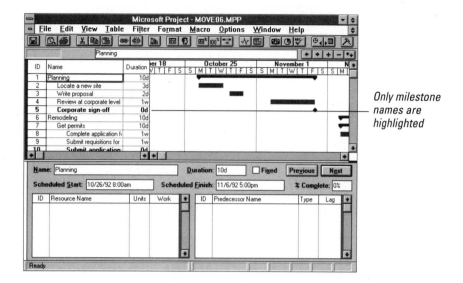

Only milestone
names are
highlighted

Creating a Custom Filter

Even though Microsoft Project supplies several filters, it is easy for you to create your own. For example, if you want to focus on tasks that start after a particular date, you can create a filter that displays (or highlights) only those tasks.

To define your own filter, choose the Define Filters command from the Filter menu. In the Filter Definition dialog box, you name the new filter and enter filter criteria. For quick access, you can add any filter you create to the Filter menu or to the tool bar. Before you apply the custom filter created in this section, you need to change the timescale of the Gantt Chart to show the effects of the filter more distinctly.

Adjusting the Timescale

Sometimes the result of applying a filter is not always clearly visible unless you change the timescale range. The timescale, located across the top of your Gantt Chart, represents the period of time during which project tasks take place. The *major timescale* on top contains larger units (in the following illustration, months). It is paired with the *minor timescale* on the bottom that contains smaller units (in this illustration, weeks).

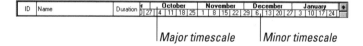

Major timescale   *Minor timescale*

Zoom In button

With the Timescale Zoom In and Timescale Zoom Out buttons on the tool bar, you can adjust the timescale units to give you more or less detail.

For example, each time you click the Timescale Zoom Out button, the size of the units increases to give you a "bigger picture" of the project. Each time you click the Timescale Zoom In button, the size of the units decreases, giving you greater detail.

Change the units on the timescale

Your screen display currently shows weeks as the major timescale and days as the minor timescale. Change the units on the timescale to show a broader range of time—months and weeks—so all the milestones appear together on the bar chart and the printout.

Zoom Out button

▶   Click the Timescale Zoom Out button on the tool bar twice to increase the units on the timescale.

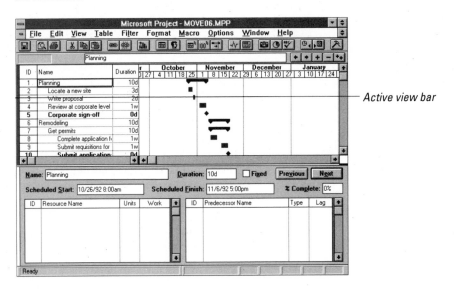

—— *Active view bar*

Print the active view

Microsoft Project prints only the active view of your project. The active view is indicated by the active view bar on the left side of the screen. Your printout won't include the Task Form that currently appears at the bottom of your screen.

If your computer is connected to a printer, you can print the view. If not, you can still see the view in Print Preview mode.

Print Preview button

1   Click the Print Preview button on the tool bar.

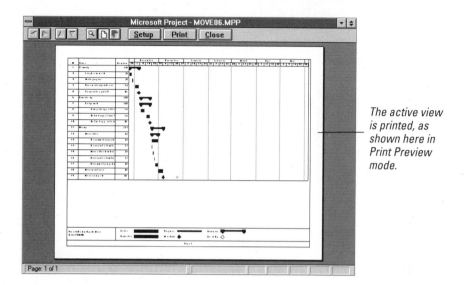

The active view
is printed, as
shown here in
Print Preview
mode.

2   If you are connected to a printer, choose the Print button. If you are not connected to a printer, choose the Close button.

Microsoft Project prints the Gantt Chart you see on your screen. You'll learn more about printing in Lesson 16, "Printing Views and Reports."

Name a custom filter

To assist you in the Victory Sports move project, the branch manager has offered to assign another assistant to you for three weeks starting November 1. You can create a custom filter to check the tasks occurring on or after November 1 and see what jobs need the most work.

Create a filter that displays all tasks starting on or after November 1.

1   From the Filter menu, choose Define Filters.

2   Choose the New button.

The Filter Definition dialog box appears. You enter filter criteria in appropriate fields of this dialog box.

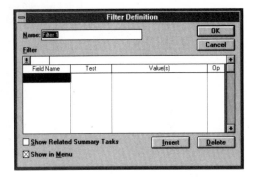

3 In the Name box, type **On or After 11/1**

Enter the filter criteria

You can also press TAB to move from field to field.

1 Click the Field Name field.

2 Click the entry bar arrow to display the list of fields.

3 Select Scheduled Start from the list.

You might need to scroll down to locate the field.

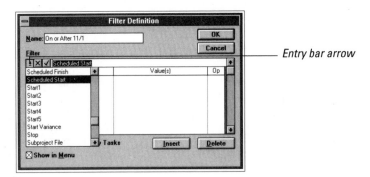

Entry bar arrow

4 Move to the Test column.

5 Click the entry bar arrow to display the list of tests.

6 Select Gtr Or Equal from the list.

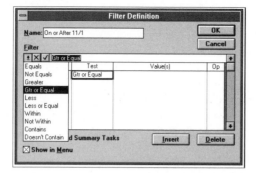

7   Move to the Value(s) column and type **11/1/92**

You can clear the check box if you don't want to add a filter to the menu.

8   Click the enter box on the entry bar or press ENTER.

In the lower-left corner of the dialog box, the Show In Menu check box is already selected, so the filter is added to the Filter menu.

The completed dialog box looks like the following illustration.

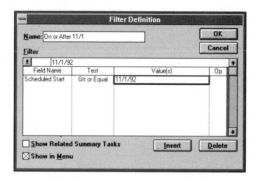

9   Click OK to return to the Define Filters dialog box.

Notice that the "On or After 11/1" filter has been added to the list of filters, and is currently selected.

10   Click the Set button to apply the filter.

Any task scheduled to start before November 1 is hidden.

Show all tasks

▶   From the Filter menu, choose All Tasks.

Save button

Save your project

▶   Click the Save button on the tool bar.

Combining Filter Criteria

Sometimes you might want to display tasks with a range of values or with specific values in two or more fields. For example, to help you focus on November's activities, you might need to display only those tasks that begin *and* end in November.

You can create filters that more precisely display exactly what you want by using the AND or OR operators. *Operators* allow you to combine filter criteria that are specified in multiple rows of the Filter box. For example, to display tasks that begin *and* end in November, you need to define and combine two filters in the Filter box. The first filter looks for tasks with a Scheduled Start date greater than 11/1/92; the second filter looks for tasks with a Scheduled Finish date less than 12/1/92. Using the AND filter operator means that both filters are in effect at the same time, so that a task must meet the criteria specified in both filters to be displayed.

Add an operator to a filter

1   From the Filter menu, choose Define Filters.

    The Define Filters dialog box appears.

2   In the Filters box, select On Or After 11/1.

3   Choose the Copy button so you can work on a copy of this filter.

4   Click the Op field.

5   Click the entry bar arrow to display a list of operators.

6   Select And from the list.

Combine filter criteria

1   Click the Field Name field (below Scheduled Start)

2   Click the entry bar arrow to display a list of fields.

3   Scroll to Scheduled Finish and select it from the list.

4   Click the Test field.

5   Click the entry bar arrow to display a list of tests.

6   Scroll to Less and select it from the list.

7   In the Value(s) field, type **12/1/92**

8   Click the enter box, or press ENTER.

9   You won't use this filter often, so clear the Show In Menu check box.

    The completed dialog box looks like the following illustration.

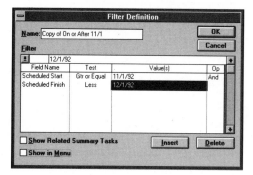

10 Choose the OK button.

11 Choose the Set button.

Microsoft Project shows only the tasks that begin and end in November. Your project looks like the following illustration.

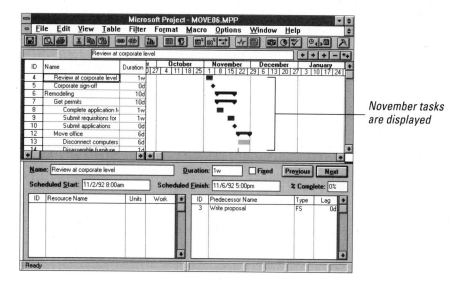

November tasks are displayed

Change the timescale

To see the timescale in more detail, change the units on the timescale back to weeks over days.

Zoom In button

1 Click the Timescale Zoom In button on the tool bar twice to decrease the size of the units on the timescale.

2   Click to the right of the horizontal scroll bar.

Microsoft Project displays the Gantt bars for tasks beginning on or after November 1, and before December 1.

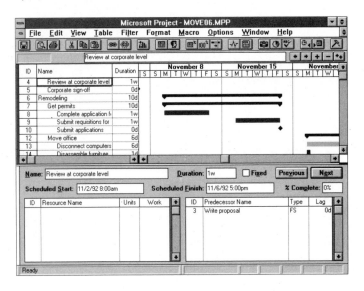

Save button

Save your project

▶   Click the Save button on the tool bar.

One Step Further

You can install a filter on the tool bar to make applying filters even easier. Then you can apply a frequently used filter with the click of a button.

Hammer button

Funnel button

1   Press CTRL while you click on the blank area to the right of the Hammer button on the tool bar.

2   Scroll through the Picture Library until you see the button that looks like a funnel.

3   Click the Funnel button to select it.

4   In the Command box, scroll through the list until you see the Filter command.

5   Click the Filter command to select it.

6   Press END to move the insertion point to the end of the word "filter."

7   Press SPACEBAR.

8   Type **[MILESTONES]**

Be sure to type the square brackets [ ].

9   Click OK.

The Funnel button appears on the end of the tool bar.

10   Apply the Milestones filter by clicking the new button you placed on the tool bar.

11   To display all the tasks again, from the Filter menu, choose All Tasks.

Because you don't need this button in future lessons, remove the button from the tool bar.

Funnel button

Remove the new button

▶   While pressing the SHIFT key, point to the Funnel button, and then drag the button down and off the tool bar.

If You Want to Continue to the Next Lesson

Save and close your project file

1   From the File menu, choose Close.

2   Choose the Yes button if you see the message box asking whether you want to save your work.

If You Want to Quit Microsoft Project for Now

Save and quit Microsoft Project

1   From the File menu, choose Exit.

2   Choose the Yes button if you see the message box asking whether you want to save your work.

Lesson Summary

To	Do this
Apply a display filter	Select a filter from the Filter menu.
Apply a highlighting filter	Hold down the SHIFT key and select a filter from the Filter menu.
Create a filter	Choose the Define Filters command from the Filter menu. Choose the Edit button to modify an existing filter. Choose the Copy button to make a new filter based on an existing one. Choose the New button to create a filter not based on a currently defined filter.
Change the timescale	Click the Timescale Zoom In and Timescale Zoom Out buttons on the tool bar.

For more information, see in the *Microsoft Project User's Reference*

Custom Edit Forms   73

Filter Commands   129

Filters   131

For an online lesson, see in the Microsoft Project for Windows Online Tutorial

Emphasizing Information

Preview of the Next Lesson

Another way to organize your project data is to sort it in a way that makes sense to you. In the next lesson, you'll learn how to use Microsoft Project to sort data, so that you can get even greater control over how you view and use project information. Combined with filters and outlining, sorting is a powerful feature in helping you work with Microsoft Project.

Sorting Project Tasks

In this lesson, you'll learn to use sorting as a quick and easy way to rearrange a project's tasks. You'll sort by a single field, Duration, to rearrange tasks by length. Combining the result with a second sort field, Scheduled Start, will let you evaluate which tasks start first and are most time consuming.

You will learn how to:

- Sort tasks using one field.

- Sort tasks using multiple fields.

Estimated lesson time: 30 minutes

Start Microsoft Project

If you closed Microsoft Project in the last lesson, restart the application now.

▶ Double-click the Microsoft Project icon.

Start the lesson

Follow these steps to open the project file called PRACT07.MPP and rename it MOVE07.MPP.

1 From the File menu, choose Open.

2 In the Directories box, double-click PRACTICE.

3 In the File Name box, double-click PRACT07.MPP.

4 From the File menu, choose Save As.

5 In the File Name box, type **MOVE07.MPP**

6 Choose the OK button.

Microsoft Project stores your project on your hard disk with the filename MOVE07.MPP.

7 Press ALT+HOME to set the timescale at the beginning of the project.

Sorting Tasks

By default, Microsoft Project lists tasks and resources in ascending (smallest to largest) order by ID number. When you sort a project, you rearrange the tasks or resources by specifying which fields the program should use to list them. With the Sort command on the Format menu you sort a project using up to three fields or *keys*.

The sort order is saved with each view, so the next time you use the view, Microsoft Project sorts the project according to the sort order in effect when you last saved the view. Sorting does not change the Task ID number. However, if you prefer the new sort order to the original one, you can choose the Renumber button in the Sort dialog box to renumber the Task IDs to reflect the new sort order.

Ascending and Descending Sort Orders

If you are sorting a task view, the list of keys includes all available task fields by which you can sort.

Microsoft Project can sort tasks in ascending or descending order. When a key is a text field, it is sorted in ascending order from 0 through 9, and then A through Z. Descending order is sorted from Z through A, and then 9 through 0. Microsoft Project ignores case when sorting text; uppercase and lowercase letters are sorted together.

When a key is a date field, Microsoft Project sorts tasks in ascending order from the earliest date to the latest date. Select the Descending option button in the Sort dialog box to sort from the latest date to the earliest date.

When a key is a numeric field, Microsoft Project sorts tasks in ascending order from the lowest number to the highest number. Select the Descending option button in the Sort dialog box to sort from the highest number to the lowest number.

Display the Task Sheet in a full screen view

▶ Hold down SHIFT and open the View menu; then choose Task Sheet

Pressing SHIFT when you select a view from the View menu displays the view in full-screen, single view. Your project looks like the following illustration.

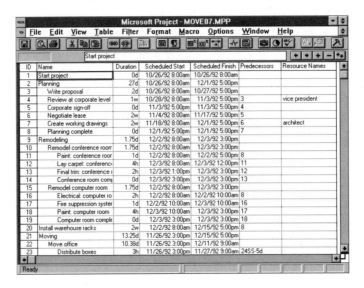

Sort the task list by duration

The tasks are currently listed in ascending order of ID number—the order in which you entered them. Follow these steps to sort tasks using the Duration field as the key.

1 From the Format menu, choose Sort.

The Sort dialog box appears.

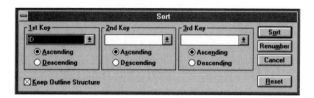

2 Click the 1st Key box arrow to display a list of task field names.

A list of task field names appears.

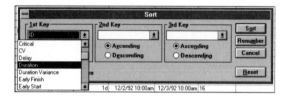

3 Select Duration.

Duration appears in the 1st Key box. The Ascending option button in the 1st Key box should be selected to sort group names in ascending order, from shortest duration to longest.

4 Choose the Sort button.

The tasks are sorted in ascending order according to the contents of the Duration field. Now you can easily spot all the tasks that require the least or greatest amount of time to accomplish.

Your project looks like the following illustration.

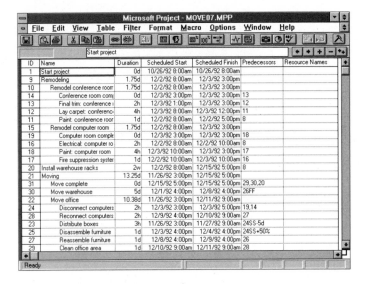

ID	Name	Duration	Scheduled Start	Scheduled Finish	Predecessors	Resource Names
1	Start project	0d	10/26/92 8:00am	10/26/92 8:00am		
9	Remodeling	1.75d	12/2/92 8:00am	12/3/92 3:00pm		
10	Remodel conference room	1.75d	12/2/92 8:00am	12/3/92 3:00pm		
14	Conference room comp	0d	12/3/92 3:00pm	12/3/92 3:00pm	13	
13	Final trim: conference r	2h	12/3/92 1:00pm	12/3/92 3:00pm	12	
12	Lay carpet: conference	4h	12/3/92 8:00am	12/3/92 12:00pm	11	
11	Paint: conference room	1d	12/2/92 8:00am	12/2/92 5:00pm	8	
15	Remodel computer room	1.75d	12/2/92 8:00am	12/3/92 3:00pm		
19	Computer room comple	0d	12/3/92 3:00pm	12/3/92 3:00pm	18	
16	Electrical: computer ro	2h	12/2/92 8:00am	12/2/92 10:00am	8	
18	Paint: computer room	4h	12/3/92 10:00am	12/3/92 3:00pm	17	
17	Fire suppression system	1d	12/2/92 10:00am	12/3/92 10:00am	16	
20	Install warehouse racks	2w	12/2/92 8:00am	12/15/92 5:00pm	8	
21	Moving	13.25d	11/26/92 3:00pm	12/15/92 5:00pm		
31	Move complete	0d	12/15/92 5:00pm	12/15/92 5:00pm	29,30,20	
30	Move warehouse	5d	12/1/92 4:00pm	12/8/92 4:00pm	26FF	
22	Move office	10.38d	11/26/92 3:00pm	12/11/92 9:00am		
24	Disconnect computers	2h	12/3/92 3:00pm	12/3/92 5:00pm	19,14	
28	Reconnect computers	2h	12/9/92 4:00pm	12/10/92 9:00am	27	
23	Distribute boxes	3h	11/26/92 3:00pm	11/27/92 9:00am	24SS-5d	
25	Disassemble furniture	1d	12/3/92 4:00pm	12/4/92 4:00pm	24SS+50%	
27	Reassemble furniture	1d	12/8/92 4:00pm	12/9/92 4:00pm	26	
29	Clean office area	1d	12/10/92 9:00am	12/11/92 9:00am	28	

Sorting an Outlined Project

As you have learned, when you apply a filter or collapse part of an outline, some tasks are hidden from view. When you sort a filtered or collapsed task list, the outline structure is retained and the tasks remain only if the Keep Outline Structure check box is selected. (In the Sort dialog box, the Keep Outline Structure check box is selected by default.)

If you clear the Keep Outline Structure check box, your task list is sorted without regard to outline structure. Once the outline no longer has its original structure, you cannot change the structure of the outline. This means that the outline buttons on the outline tool bar are disabled, and you cannot promote, demote, collapse, or expand tasks. If you want to use the outline buttons, you first need to return the task list to its original order by choosing the Reset button in the Sort dialog box.

Save button

Save your project

▶ Click the Save button on the tool bar.

Sorting by Multiple Keys

Another way to tap the power of sorting is to sort by two or more keys. By specifying two keys by which you want to sort, Microsoft Project first sorts by the first key, and then sorts the tasks again within each grouping by the second key. For example, if your first key is Duration and the second key is Scheduled Start, Microsoft Project sorts the tasks, so the tasks that require the same amount of time are grouped together. Then the tasks are sorted by their scheduled start date within each group.

Sort the task list by Duration and Scheduled Start

To display the range of tasks that start first and are the most time consuming, you can sort using two fields as keys. The Duration field is the first key and the Scheduled Start field is the second key.

1 From the Format menu, choose Sort.

The Sort dialog box appears. Notice that the 1st Key box retains the sort field from your previous sort.

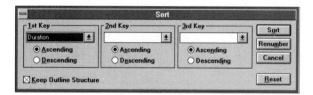

2 Under 1st Key, select the Descending option button.

3 Click the arrow next to the 2nd Key box to display the list.

4 Select Scheduled Start, and be sure Ascending is selected under 2nd Key.

5 Choose the Sort button.

Microsoft Project sorts tasks in descending order from longest to shortest duration. Those tasks with the same durations are in turn sorted according to the Scheduled Start field. Your project looks like the following illustration.

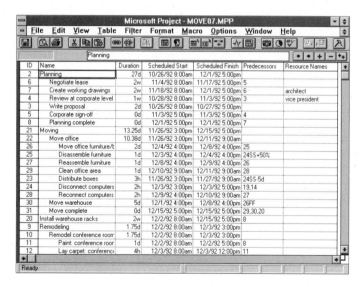

Reset the task list to ID number order

Now you've sorted information on one key and on multiple keys. Your new sort order replaces the previous one. Next you return your task list to ascending order by ID number.

1   From the Format menu, choose <u>S</u>ort.

2   Choose the Reset button to return the task list to ID number order.

3   Choose the Sort button.

Now the Task Sheet displays tasks in the order in which you entered them.

Save button

Save your project

▶   Click the Save button on the tool bar.

Sorting an Updated Project

When you edit the task list by adding, deleting, or moving tasks, Microsoft Project does not automatically re-sort the task list. You need to rearrange the updated task list to reflect the sort order you want. To do this, simply choose Sort from the Format menu again. Because you probably want to retain the same sort order, don't change the current settings in the Sort dialog box. When you choose the Sort button, the task list is sorted again, this time incorporating your latest changes.

One Step Further

When specifying a sort order in the steps throughout this lesson, you retained the structure of the outline. Explore the effect of clearing the Keep Outline Structure check box. Sort the tasks in ascending order by start date.

1   From the Format menu, choose <u>S</u>ort.

2   Click the 1st Key box arrow to display a list of task field names.

3   Select Scheduled Start.

4   Click the Keep Outline Structure check box to clear it.

5   Choose the Sort button.

The tasks are sorted in ascending order according to start date without regard to their summary tasks.

Notice that the outline buttons on the outline tool bar are disabled. With the outline no longer in its original structure, you cannot change the hierarchy of the task list.

6   From the Format menu, choose <u>S</u>ort.

7   Choose the Reset button.

8   Choose the Sort button to return the task list to its original sort order.

If You Want to Continue to the Next Lesson

Save and close your project file

1   From the File menu, choose Close.

2   Choose the Yes button if you see the message box asking whether you want to save your work.

If You Want to Quit Microsoft Project for Now

Save and quit Microsoft Project

1   From the File menu, choose Exit.

2   Choose the Yes button if you see the message box asking whether you want to save your work.

Lesson Summary

To	Do this
Sort by a single field	Choose the Sort command from the Format menu. Select a field in the 1st Key list.
Sort by multiple fields	Choose the Sort command from the Format menu. Select fields in the 1st Key, 2nd Key, and 3rd Key lists.
Reset the task list	Choose the Sort command from the Format menu, and choose the Reset button.

For more information, see in the *Microsoft Project User's Reference*

Sorting Information   474

Preview of the Next Lesson

In the next lesson, you'll begin to learn about working with the resources in your project. Throughout the lessons in Part 3, you will focus on assigning resources to each task, scheduling resources, and determining the cost of each task (and the project).

Review & Practice

In the lessons in Part 2, "Creating a Project," you learned skills to help you enter and organize task information in a project. If you want to practice these skills and test your knowledge before you proceed with the lessons in Part 3, you can work through the Review & Practice following this lesson.

Part 2   Review & Practice

Before you begin planning a project of your own, practice the skills you learned in Part 2 by working through the project management activities in this Review & Practice section. Based on the plan you created in the Part 1 Review & Practice, you will enter tasks and durations. You will also use summary tasks to develop an outline structure. After you assign relationships, you will apply a filter to display specific tasks.

Scenario

With the broad goals and deadlines identified, your next step as the project manager for the annual report project is to specify the tasks required to complete the project. Each task takes a specific amount of time that you must supply in the project plan. To help you organize the tasks, you need to create an outline structure for the project. Use filters to focus on different kinds of tasks as they become important to you.

You will review and practice how to:

- Enter tasks and durations.
- Use summary tasks and outline the project.
- Assign relationships.
- Filter tasks based on built-in filters.

Estimated practice time: 25 minutes

Before You Begin

1 Open the scenario project called 2ANNUAL.MPP.

2 Save the project file as ANNUAL2.MPP.

This project file should look similar to the file you saved after completing the steps in Scenario 1. However, notice the addition of some new tasks.

3 Press ALT+HOME to set the timescale at the beginning of the project.

Step 1: Enter Tasks

Insert the following tasks and durations after task 15, "Write Articles."

Task	Duration
Write first draft	1d
Management review	1d
Edit	1d
Review	1d
Final edit	1d

For more information on	See
Entering tasks	Lesson 4
Summary tasks	Lesson 4

Create a Summary Task

Make "Write Articles" a summary task by demoting the new tasks you inserted.

Scroll the timescale to see the Gantt bars for these tasks.

Collapse the Entire Task List

Use the Collapse button on the tool bar to collapse the task list.

Only the first level summary tasks are displayed.

Collapse button

Expand a Task

Expand only the "Assemble final materials" summary task.

Then use the Expand All button to expand all the summary tasks.

Expand all button

Delete Tasks

Delete tasks 19 and 20 from the task list.

For more information on	See
Moving, inserting, and deleting tasks	Lesson 3
Moving, inserting, and deleting summary tasks	Lesson 4

Step 2: Assign Task Relationships

Link Tasks

Use the Link button to link the tasks 16, 17, 18, and 19 together.

Enter a Lead Time

Schedule to finish printing the cover letters and envelopes three days before the reports are due back from the service bureau. This means that for task 33, "Print covers and envelopes," you need to add a finish-to-finish relationship with the predecessor task 28. Enter a lead time of three days for task 33, depending on the finish of task 28.

For more information on	See
Linking and finish-to-start relationships	Lesson 3
Other task relationships	Lesson 5

Step 3: Organize the Project

Apply the Milestone Filter

Use the milestone filter so that the milestones are highlighted.

For more information on	See
Filters	Lesson 6

Save button

Save your project

▶ Click the Save button on the tool bar.

If You Want to Continue to the Next Lesson

Close your project file

▶ From the File menu, choose Close.

If You Want to Quit Microsoft Project for Now

Quit Microsoft Project

▶ From the File menu, choose Exit.

Part

3 Working with Resources

Managing Project Resources

In this lesson, you will learn ways to manage *resources*: the people, equipment, facilities, and supplies required to accomplish project tasks. You will enter resources in your project and assign them to tasks. Then you will assign costs to resources and view individual resources using filters.

You will learn how to:

- Enter and assign resources.
- Define a resource group name and code.
- Use a resource pool.
- Assign resource costs.
- View resource information through a filter.

Estimated lesson time: 30 minutes

Start Microsoft Project

If you closed Microsoft Project in the last lesson, you need to restart the application before you can continue.

▶ Double-click the Microsoft Project icon.

Start the lesson

Do the following to open the project file called PRACT08.MPP and rename it MOVE08.MPP.

1 From the File menu, choose Open.

2 In the Directories box, double-click PRACTICE.

3 In the File Name box, double-click PRACT08.MPP.

4 From the File menu, choose Save As.

5 In the File Name box, type **MOVE08.MPP**

6 Choose the OK button.

   Microsoft Project stores your project on your hard disk with the filename MOVE08.MPP.

7 Press ALT+HOME to set the timescale at the beginning of the project.

Assigning Resources

*Resource
Assignment button*

The fastest way to assign resources is to select a task or group of tasks and click the Resource Assignment button on the tool bar. When you assign a new resource to a task, you can add optional details about the resource, such as salary information.

When you assign a new resource to a task, its resource name is added to the *resource pool*. Once a resource is defined in the resource pool, you can assign it to any task by typing its name, or by choosing it from the list of resource names in the pool.

By default, Microsoft Project assigns one *unit* of the resource to work full time on a task. A unit can be a person, a room, a computer, or whatever constitutes a single resource assigned to that task. You can also specify a part-time resource and indicate the number of partial units of the resource you want to assign to the task. Entering resources in the resource pool this way is fast and convenient for small projects, or when you are not sure of what resources the project requires, or what resources you have available.

You can also enter a set of resources directly into the resource pool before you assign them any tasks. Use this method if you are working on a large project for which you have a known set of resources, or anticipate using the same set of resources for future projects.

Assign a resource

In the company move, your assistant entered a few of the resources for you. Take a moment to enter a few more resources. Begin by assigning yourself, as operations manager, the task of writing a proposal that describes the new office and warehouse site.

When you assign a new resource to a task, you can use the Resource Assignment dialog box to add optional details about the resource.

1   Select task 3, "Write proposal."

2   Click the Resource Assignment button on the tool bar.

*Resource
Assignment button*

3   In the Resources box, type **operations manager**

4   Choose the Add button.

A message box asks if you want to add this resource to the resource pool.

5   Choose the Yes button.

The Resource Edit Form dialog box appears.

Providing Resource Details

In the Resource Edit Form dialog box you can enter additional information about a resource. Entering resource details, such as initials, a group name, or code, allows you to take advantage of assignment shortcuts and facilitates better resource tracking.

Each resource can belong to a group. For example, John, Mary, and Joe can each be assigned to a group named "electricians." If you enter group names and codes, you can pull together reports on the costs or schedules for each group. As a result, you can filter all the resources and display information for the electricians only.

Enter initials

Using a shorter name speeds up the job of making resource assignments. The next time you need to assign this resource to a task, you can type initials instead of the entire resource name.

▶ In the Initials box, type **opm**

Use these initials whenever you assign a task to yourself, the operations manager.

The Code text box can be used for various purposes. For example, you could enter a supervisor's name in the Code box and later apply a filter for that name to see a list of everyone who works for that supervisor.

Enter a group name and code

The management at Victory Sports divides their resources into these groups: office staff, management, maintenance workers, warehouse staff, contractors, and equipment.

Assign yourself to the management group and enter an accounting code of 101-200.

1 In the Group box, type **management**

2 In the Code box, type **101-200**

3 Choose the OK button.

Using the Resource Pool

Another way to assign a resource to a task is to select names from the resource pool. When you select a blank field in the Resource Name column in the Task Form, an arrow appears in the entry bar, displaying a list of all resources available in the pool. You can select a name from the list to assign a resource to the task.

The Units field on the Task Form determines the amount of each resource assigned to the task. Part-time resources are expressed as fractions of full-time units. For example, a part-time computer programmer working 20 hours a week appears as .5 units, whereas a full-time programmer working 40 hours a week would appear as 1 unit.

Select a resource from the pool

Do the following to assign your operations assistant to help you write the proposal.

1   Select the blank field below Operations Manager in the Resource Name column.

2   Click the entry bar arrow to display the list of resources.

3   Click Operations Assistant, and then click the enter box on the entry bar.

4   Choose the OK button.

Assign a resource to several tasks

*Resource
Assignment button*

To enter resource information common to several tasks or resources, you can again use the Resource Assignment button on the tool bar or the Assignment command on the Edit menu. When you need to move to a specific task that is not currently on the screen, you can do it quickly using the Go To command on the Edit menu. With this command, you can specify the task ID you want, or you can enter the date you want displayed.

Use the Go To command on the Edit menu to quickly move to the "Move office furniture/boxes" task. Then select two other tasks and assign yourself to them.

1   Click in the Gantt Chart to make it active.

*You can also press
F5 to display the Go
To dialog box.*

2   From the Edit menu, choose Go To.

3   In the ID box, type **26**

4   Choose the OK button.

   The Go To command locates task 26.

5   Hold down CTRL, and select task 29.

   Both tasks 26 and 29 are now selected.

6   Click the Resource Assignment button on the tool bar.

7   Click the arrow to display the list of resources, and select Operations Manager from the list.

8   Choose the Add button.

   You are now assigned to work full time on both of the tasks you selected.

*Resource
Assignment button*

Add another resource to the resource pool

You currently have 15 warehouse workers on the day shift. Assign them to the task of moving the warehouse.

1   Select task 30, "Move warehouse."

2   Click the Resource Assignment button on the tool bar.

   Since you are assigning more than one worker, type the number of workers in brackets after the resource name.

*Resource
Assignment button*

3   In the Resources box, type **day warehouse workers[15]**

4   Choose the Add button.

5   Choose the Yes button to add this resource.

The Resource Edit Form dialog box appears.

6   In the Initials box, type **dww**

7   In the Max Units box, type **15**

Microsoft Project uses this limit for determining when the resources are overscheduled.

Keep the Resource Edit Form dialog box on the screen to enter resource costs in the following exercises.

Working with Costs

Costs can be *fixed* or *variable*. Contractors, for example, often bid a fixed price for a job, meaning the cost remains the same even if the task takes more or less time than planned. Variable costs, on the other hand, typically include people and equipment that incur costs over time or per use.

Microsoft Project offers three cost accrual methods, which you can choose from the "Accrue At" list box.

Start   Select Start as the accrual method if costs accrue as soon as a task using the resource begins.

End   Select End as the accrual method if costs do not accrue until after the task finishes. Fixed costs for tasks are always accrued at the end of each task.

Prorated   Choose to *prorate* the cost when costs accrue as the task using the resource progresses, based on the work done. Prorated is the default accrual method.

Enter an hourly rate

The warehouse workers normally earn $8 per hour. Their overtime rate is $12 per hour. Enter these standard and overtime rates.

You can press TAB to move from field to field in the form.

1   In the Std Rate box, type **$8/h**

2   In the Ovt Rate box, type **$12/h**

3   In the Group box, type **warehouse**

4   In the Code box, type **301-110**

This code is the Victory Sports accounting code for the warehouse workers. You can filter and sort on group and code information to get useful reports about groups of resources.

5   Choose the OK button.

Assign a resource with a fixed cost

The carpet contractor gives you a fixed price of $1,275 for carpeting the conference room. After you assign the carpet contractor to task 12, "Lay carpet: conference room," enter the fixed cost of installing the carpet. Use the Go To command on the Edit menu to locate the task quickly.

1   Click in the Gantt Chart to make it active.

2   From the Edit menu, choose Go To.

3   In the ID box, type **12**

4   Choose the OK button.

5   Click the Resource Assignment button on the tool bar.

6   In the Resources box, type **carpet contractor**

7   Choose the Add button.

8   Choose the Yes button.

    The Resource Edit Form dialog box appears.

9   In the Initials box, type **cc**

10   In the Group box, type **contractor**

11   In the Code box, type **501-102**

    This is the Victory Sports accounting code for this kind of contractor.

12   Choose the OK button.

Enter a fixed cost

To enter fixed costs, you first need to apply the Cost table to the Gantt Chart. Then you can enter fixed costs in the Fixed Cost field.

1   From the Table menu, choose Cost.

    Choosing the Cost command displays a table for entering and viewing cost information. You can drag the vertical divider bar to the right to see more of the data in the table.

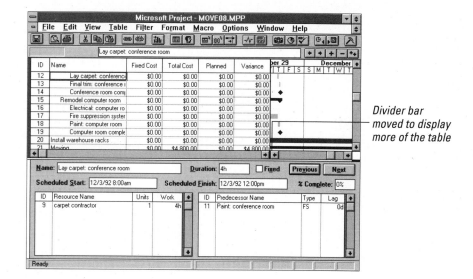

Divider bar moved to display more of the table

2 In the Fixed Cost column, click the field for Task 12 to select it.

3 Type **1275**

4 Click the enter box on the entry bar or press ENTER.

Viewing Resources

You can see all the people and equipment in the resource pool with the Resource Sheet. With its spreadsheet-like format, the Resource Sheet is a convenient way to review many resources at once. Change to the Resource Sheet view of the project and look for the resources you have added.

View the resource pool

▶ Hold down SHIFT and choose Resource Sheet from the View menu for a single-pane view.

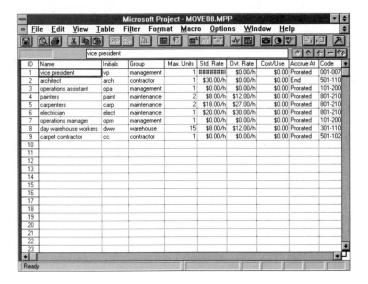

Number signs (##) appearing in any field indicate that the value is too large for
that field's column width. Double-click the column heading to the right of the
column name to change the column width to the best size for the information in the
column.

Filter on a group name

It's also easy to filter, sort, and change resource information in this view. What other
managers have been entered in this resource pool? Microsoft Project supplies a filter
that displays only the members of the group you specify. Use the next steps to filter
the resource pool so only members of the management group are displayed.

*If you want to
highlight the
management
resources rather
than hide the other
resources, hold
down SHIFT in step 1.*

1   From the File menu, choose Group.

2   In the Group Name box, type **management**

3   Choose the OK button.

All resources in the management group are displayed. The other resources are
hidden. Your Resource Sheet looks like the following illustration.

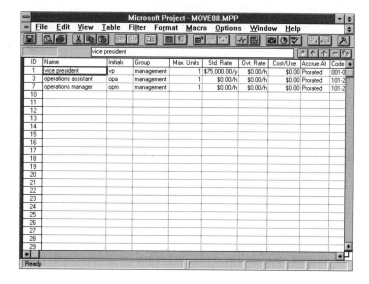

Save button

Save your project

▶ Click the Save button on the tool bar.

One Step Further

The corporate office of Victory Sports has just changed the accounting code for all maintenance workers. Enter the new code, 601-210, for each resource in the maintenance group.

1 Filter the resources to display only the maintenance group.

2 Select all the resources in this group.

Form button

3 Click the Form button on the tool bar to display the Resource Edit Form dialog box.

4 In the Code box, type **601-210**

5 Choose the OK button.

The new code number appears for all the maintenance workers.

If You Want to Continue to the Next Lesson

Save and close your project file

1 From the File menu, choose Close.

2 Choose the Yes button if you see the message box asking whether you want to save your work.

If You Want to Quit Microsoft Project for Now

Save and quit Microsoft Project

1   From the File menu, choose Exit.

2   Choose the Yes button if you see the message box asking whether you want to save your work.

Lesson Summary

To	Do this
Enter and assign resources	Assign a resource to the selected task by entering a resource name in the Resource Name field in the Task Form or in the Resources Task Sheet.
Assign resource costs	Enter costs for a selected resource in the Std. Rate, Ovt. Rate and Accrue fields on the Resource Sheet. These fields are also on the Resource Edit Form. You can display the Resource Edit Form by double-clicking a resource.
Enter a group name and code	Enter group name and code information for a selected resource in the Resource Sheet Group and Code fields. These fields are also on the Resource Edit Form. You can display the Resource Edit Form by double-clicking on a resource.
Filter resource information	With a resource view selected, choose a filter from the Filter menu.

For more information, see in the *Microsoft Project User's Reference*

Assigning Resources   3

Entering Resources   106

Task Form   517

For an online lesson, see in the Microsoft Project for Windows Online Tutorial

Entering Resources

Managing Resources

Preview of the Next Lesson

Coordinating the schedules of your resources can be a juggling act. Microsoft Project has a calendar system that does the trick by scheduling each task when the resources are available. In next lesson, you'll learn several ways to enter exceptions to the standard Monday through Friday, 8:00 A.M. to 5:00 A.M. calendar.

Using Calendars

In this lesson you will work with calendars by adjusting the standard calendar and making new base calendars. Using multiple calendars, Microsoft Project can schedule tasks in a way that reflects the individual schedules of your resources.

You will learn how to:

- Change the standard workdays.
- Change the standard work hours.
- Set holidays.
- Create new base calendars.
- Edit resource calendars.

Estimated lesson time: 30 minutes

Start Microsoft Project

If you closed Microsoft Project in the last lesson, you need to restart the application before you can continue.

▶ Double-click the Microsoft Project icon.

Start the lesson

Follow these steps to open the project file called PRACT09.MPP and rename it MOVE09.MPP.

1 From the File menu, choose Open.

2 In the Directories box, double-click PRACTICE.

3 In the File Name box, double-click PRACT09.MPP.

4 From the File menu, choose Save As.

5 In the File Name box, type **MOVE09.MPP**

6 Choose the OK button.

Microsoft Project stores your project on your hard disk with the filename MOVE09.MPP.

7 Press ALT+HOME to set the timescale at the beginning of the project.

Changing Calendars

There are two types of calendars: *base* calendars and *resource* calendars. A base calendar defines the usual working and nonworking days and hours for the project or a group of resources. A resource calendar defines working and nonworking days for a specific resource or group of resources whose availability does not conform to the base calendar.

The default base calendar, called Standard, shows a Monday through Friday work-week, from 8:00 A.M. to 5:00 P.M., with an hour off at noon and no holidays. You must specify all nonworking days, even official, national holidays. Use the Project Info command on the Options menu to select a base calendar for the project.

A resource calendar contains the usual working and nonworking days and hours for the resource. But it also specifies unique exceptions, such as vacations, part-time hours, or regular overtime.

Using Base Calendars

Use base calendars for groups of resources. For example, if several resources work part time from 8:00 A.M. to 12:00 P.M., you can create a second base calendar that shows these hours. You can have more than one base calendar in your project. You can give the new base calendar a name such as "Part-time" and use it with other projects as well.

When you edit a base calendar, any changes you make are reflected in the resource calendars that depend on that base calendar. Choosing the Reset button makes the base calendar identical to the Standard calendar.

Using Resource Calendars

Use the resource calendar for individual resources. Although resource calendars begin as exact copies of the Standard calendar, you can select a different base calendar and then easily customize each resource calendar to show the resource's personal vacation days, time away from the office, or individual work hours. In the case of equipment, a resource calendar can reflect scheduled maintenance, downtime, or any other exception to the normal schedule.

In a resource calendar, select the Default option button to change selected days to match the working or nonworking status for that day in the base calendar.

Change the workweek

An independent consulting company recommends that Victory Sports change to a four-day workweek to achieve a substantial savings on utilities. Most employees would work Tuesday through Friday. Change the Standard calendar to show the schedule most resources would have if the workweek changes.

1   From the Options menu, choose Base Calendars.

Note that the Standard base calendar is selected. This is the default base calendar.

2   Choose the Edit button.

3   Click M in the day titles to select all Mondays.

4   Select the Nonworking option button.

All Mondays appear gray, indicating that they are nonworking days. The Hours boxes show working hours for the selected day; since Monday is a nonworking day, the Hours boxes are blank.

Your calendar looks like the following illustration.

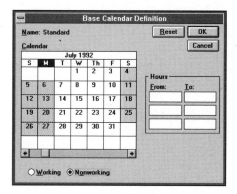

Change the working hours

Set the hours so you still have 40-hour weeks. The hours would be 7:00 A.M. to 6:00 P.M., with an hour for lunch at 11:30 A.M. Because these hours affect all four days, first select all four day titles, and then change the hours.

1   Drag the mouse across the Tuesday through Friday day titles to select them.

The working hours for these days appear in the Hours boxes.

2   Click the first From box under Hours.

3   Type the following times.

From: To:

7:00 am   11:30 am

Press TAB to move between boxes. If you make a mistake and need to move back to a previous box, press SHIFT+TAB.

4   Press TAB to move to the second From box under Hours.

5 Type the following times.

From: **To:**

12:30 pm   6:00 pm

Your calendar looks like the following illustration.

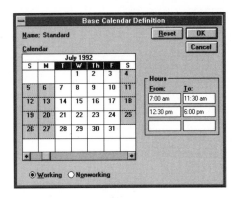

6 Choose the OK button.

7 Choose the Close button.

Microsoft Project reschedules the project using a Tuesday through Friday work-week.

Save button

Save your project

▶ Click the Save button on the tool bar.

Reset the Standard base calendar

The executive board has rejected the new workweek proposal. Reset the Standard base calendar.

1 From the Options menu, choose Base Calendars.

2 Choose the Edit button.

3 Choose the Reset button.

4 Choose the Yes button.

Set a holiday

The annual company meeting is on October 14. You need to make this a nonworking day in the Standard calendar.

1 Click an arrow at the base of the calendar to move to October 1992.

2 Select October 14.

3 Select the Nonworking option button.

October 14 turns gray to indicate it is now a nonworking day. The working hours for this day are deleted from the Hours boxes.

Your calendar looks like the following illustration.

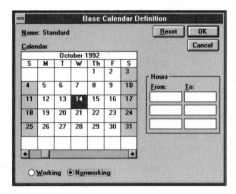

4 Choose the OK button to return to the Base Calendars dialog box.

5 Choose the Save button to save these changes.

6 Choose the OK button to save the changes in a calendar file.

Your Standard calendar now includes the company meeting as a nonworking day.

Microsoft Project stores the calendar in a file called CALENDAR.MPC. This standard calendar file is shared among projects that you use with Microsoft Project on your computer.

Creating a New Base Calendar

You have three resources that work at night: the night warehouse supervisor, the night warehouse workers, and the janitors. They work the same workweek and observe the same days off, but their hours are different. You need to prepare a new base calendar to reflect their hours.

Copy a base calendar

To minimize the amount of editing you have to do, make a copy of the Standard calendar. The days and holidays are already set. Then, when you edit this copy, you change only the hours for these workers.

▶ Choose the Copy button.

A copy of the Standard calendar appears, ready for editing.

Change the working hours

Do the following to set the hours for the night crews. Since the night shift spans more than one calendar day, enter the hours before midnight on one day and the hours after midnight on the next day.

1   Select the Monday day title.

2   In the Hours boxes, type the following times.

From:	To:
6:00 pm	10:00 pm
10:30 pm	12:00 am

The night crew has a half-hour break from 10:00 P.M. to 10:30 P.M.

Press TAB to move between boxes. If you make a mistake and need to move back to a previous box, press SHIFT +TAB.

3   Select the Tuesday through Friday day titles.

4   In the Hours boxes, type the following times.

From:	To:
12:00 am	2:30 am
6:00 pm	10:00 pm
10:30 pm	12:00 am

5   Select the Saturday day title.

6   In the Hours boxes, type the following times.

From:	To:
12:00 am	2:30 am

7   At the bottom of the dialog box, select the Working option button.

Your calendar looks like the following illustration.

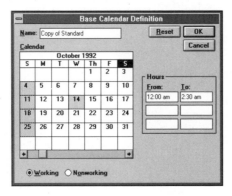

Name the new base calendar

In the Base Calendars dialog box Microsoft Project suggests "Copy of Standard" for the name of the calendar. Replace the suggested name with "Night Shift."

1   Select the text in the Name box, and type **Night Shift**

2   Choose the OK button.

"Night Shift" appears in the list of available base calendars.

3   Choose the Save button to save the new calendar.

4   In the next dialog box, choose the OK button to save this new calendar in the calendar file called CALENDAR.MPC.

5   In the Base Calendars dialog box, choose the Close button.

You now have two base calendars for your project: one for day workers (called Standard) and another one for night workers (called Night Shift). Both are stored in the CALENDAR.MPC calendar file on your computer.

Save button

Save your project

▶   Click the Save button on the tool bar.

Assigning Resources to a New Calendar

Microsoft Project assigns all the resources in this project to the Standard calendar. Use the next steps to assign the night warehouse workers and the janitors to the Night Shift calendar.

Reassign Resources

You can use the Form button on the tool bar to make one entry apply to several resources.

1   Hold down SHIFT and choose Resource Sheet from the View menu.

2   Select janitors, and hold down CTRL as you select the night warehouse supervisor and night warehouse workers.

Form button

3   Click the Form button on the tool bar.

4   In the Base Cal box, select Night Shift from the list.

5   Choose the OK button.

These three resources are now scheduled according to the days and hours on the Night Shift base calendar. All other resources use the default base calendar called Standard.

Save button

Save your project

▶   Click the Save button on the tool bar.

Edit a resource calendar

The night warehouse workers are scheduled to attend a safety seminar from 6:00 P.M. to midnight, November 9. They will not be available for work at that time. Enter this exception to the Night Shift calendar on the resource calendar for the night warehouse workers.

To see a resource calendar for a different resource, select the resource from the list in the Resource box.

1 Select night warehouse workers.

2 From the Options menu, choose Resource Calendars.

The resource calendar for the night warehouse workers appears.

3 Click the right arrow at the base of the calendar to move to November 1992.

4 Select November 9, 1992.

5 Select the Nonworking option button.

This nonworking day overrides the hours set on the assigned base calendar. The night warehouse workers are not scheduled to work from 6:00 P.M. to 12:00 A.M. on November 9.

Your calendar looks like the following illustration.

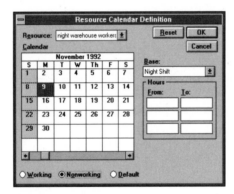

6 Choose the OK button.

Microsoft Project reschedules the tasks around the resources' nonworking days.

Save button

Save your project

▶ Click the Save button on the tool bar.

One Step Further

Set the national holidays in a new calendar, so that these holidays do not affect the scheduling of this project.

1 From the Options menu, choose Base Calendars.

The Base Calendars dialog box appears.

2   Choose the New button.

The Base Calendar Definition dialog box appears.

3   Scroll to November and make the fourth Thursday a nonworking day.

4   In the Name box, type a name for your calendar.

5   Since we do not need this calendar for future exercises, choose the Cancel button when you have finished.

6   Choose the Cancel button.

If You Want to Continue to the Next Lesson

Save and close your project file

1   From the File menu, choose Close.

2   Choose the Yes button if you see the message box asking whether you want to save your work.

If You Want to Quit Microsoft Project for Now

Save and quit Microsoft Project

1   From the File menu, choose Exit.

2   Choose the Yes button if you see the message box asking whether you want to save your work.

Lesson Summary

To	Do This
Change the standard workdays	Choose the Base Calendars command from the Options menu to access the base calendars. Select the base calendar you want to change. Select the day of the week you wish to change. Then select the Working or Nonworking button.
Change the standard work hours	Choose the Base Calendars command from the Options menu to access the base calendars. Select the base calendar you want to change. Then select the days of the week you wish to change. Enter the working hours in the Hours boxes.
Set holidays	Choose the Base Calendars command from the Options menu to access the base calendars. Select the base calendar you want to change. Select the specific days in the month you want to change. Then select the Nonworking button.

To	Do This
Create new base calendars	Choose the Base Calendars command from the Options menu to access the base calendars. Choose the Copy button to make a new calendar based on an existing one. Choose the New button to create a calendar not based on an existing calendar.
Edit resource calendar	Choose the Resource Calendars from the Options menu to display the calendar for a selected resource.

For more information, see in the *Microsoft Project User's Reference*

Calendars   15

Tracking Progress   567

For an online lesson, see in the Microsoft Project for Windows Online Tutorial

Creating Calendars

Preview of the Next Lesson

In the next lesson, you will learn to specify both *resource-driven* scheduling, where availability of resources controls the schedule, and *fixed-duration* scheduling, where time controls the schedule regardless of the resources assigned.

Scheduling with Resources

In this lesson, you will learn to alter a schedule by varying the quantity of resources used. You will also work with situations where time—rather than resources—becomes the controlling factor in project completion.

You will learn how to:

- Use resource-driven scheduling.
- Use fixed-duration scheduling.

Estimated lesson time: 40 minutes

Start Microsoft Project

If you closed Microsoft Project in the last lesson, you need to restart the application before you can continue.

▶ Double-click the Microsoft Project icon.

Start the lesson

Follow these steps to open the project file called PRACT10.MPP and rename it MOVE10.MPP.

1 From the File menu, choose Open.

2 In the Directories box, double-click PRACTICE.

3 In the File Name box, double-click PRACT10.MPP.

4 From the File menu, choose Save As.

5 In the File Name box, type **MOVE10.MPP**

6 Choose the OK button.

   Microsoft Project stores your project on your hard disk with the filename MOVE10.MPP.

7 Press ALT+HOME to set the timescale at the beginning of the project.

Note The message "Level: day warehouse workers" appears at the bottom of your screen. This means that this resource is overallocated; you'll examine the workload for this resource in Lesson 11, "Resource Workloads."

Establishing a Scheduling Method

Microsoft Project provides two scheduling methods: *resource–driven* and *fixed-duration*. The default setting provides resource-driven tasks, whose duration depends on the resources applied. There are times, however, when adding resources will not affect task duration. Such tasks are called fixed-duration tasks. The section which follows will help you understand your scheduling options in using these two types of scheduling.

Resource-Driven Scheduling

If you want resource assignments to determine the duration and the start and finish dates of a task, use resource-driven scheduling. With resource-driven scheduling, the task duration is based on the amount of work and the number of resource units assigned to a task. Resource calendars determine the start and finish dates for the task.

For example, suppose the "Move warehouse" task has two movers assigned. With resource-driven scheduling, if you assign another mover, Microsoft Project shortens the task duration. The start and finish dates are determined by when the movers are available.

Resource-driven scheduling is helpful when you have limited resources to share among tasks. As you move resources from one task to another, or split resources' time between tasks, Microsoft Project gives you instant updates on how long each task will take with the current number of resources.

In earlier lessons, you entered durations for your tasks, based on your estimate of the total work for the amount of resources you plan to assign. For instance, if you estimate that a plumbing task takes three plumbers 10 hours to complete, enter a task duration of 10 hours.

Fixed-Duration Scheduling

Select fixed-duration scheduling when you want a duration to remain unchanged, or if you want to estimate the duration yourself. You can still assign resources to tasks, but Microsoft Project won't change the duration as you adjust resource assignments.

For example, you may know that it takes two hours to drive a truckload of office furniture 50 miles. No matter how many workers you assign to make the trip, the task duration remains two hours. In this case, using fixed-duration scheduling ensures that your task duration remains the same regardless of the resource assignments you make.

Changing Resource Quantities

Resource-driven scheduling is Microsoft Project's default scheduling method; each task you enter is initially set as resource-driven. You can change the scheduling method for a task on the Task Form or in the Task Edit Form dialog box by selecting or clearing the Fixed check box. To change the scheduling method for a group of selected tasks, use the Task Edit Form dialog box.

With either scheduling method, there are three important scheduling fields in the Task Form.

Duration   This field indicates how long a task takes to complete.

Work   This field contains the total effort to complete a task. It is the duration multiplied by the number of resources assigned to a task.

Units   This field is the amount of a resource you assign to a task, such as three carpenters or one engineer.

Note   You can change the default scheduling method for *all* new tasks with the Preferences command on the Options menu. In the Preferences dialog box, set the Default Duration Type option to Fixed or Not Fixed. Changing the default scheduling method affects only new tasks—not tasks you've already entered.

Display the details of a resource-driven task

The day warehouse supervisor estimates it takes two weeks for 8 of the 15 day warehouse workers to install inventory racks in the new warehouse. The supervisor needs to oversee the work as well.

From the Task Entry view, select the "Install warehouse racks" task to display the details in the Task Form.

1   Select task 20, "Install warehouse racks."

   Note that the Fixed check box in the Task Form is cleared, which means the task uses resource-driven scheduling.

2   Scroll the Gantt chart to the week of November 29

   The bar for task 20 will be visible.

Change units of an assigned resource

Working full time for two weeks, eight day warehouse workers work a total of 640 hours (10 days x 8 hours/day x 8 workers = 640 hours).

Now that you know how much work the task requires, you can use resource-driven scheduling to quickly test some "what if" scenarios. You can use Microsoft Project to see how changing the resource assignments affects the duration of this task.

You need to shorten the task to a week so you can start the warehouse move earlier. Try doubling the number of day warehouse workers.

1   Move to the Task Form.

2   Select the Units field for day warehouse workers.

3   Type **16**

4   Choose the OK button.

   The duration changes from two weeks (2w) to one week (1w).

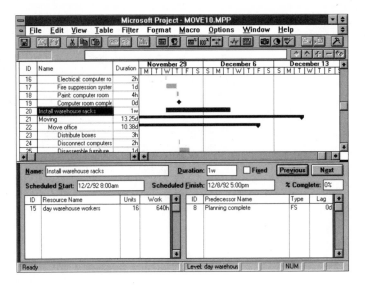

Save button

Save your project

▶ Click the Save button on the tool bar.

Assigning Multiple Resources to One Task

If two different resources are assigned to the same task, Microsoft Project calculates the duration as the largest amount of work per unit done by any one resource. For example, if a piece of equipment must run for two hours, while a laboratory researcher works three hours on the same task, the task duration is three hours. However, if you add a second researcher, thus reducing the hours per researcher to 1.5 hours, the task duration for the piece of equipment is two hours.

Add another resource to the task

Now that you've reduced the duration of the "Install warehouse racks" task, assign the day warehouse supervisor to the task while the day warehouse workers are at the warehouse.

Resource Assignment button

1 Click the Resource Assignment button on the tool bar.

2 In the Resources box, select day warehouse supervisor from the list.

3 Choose the Add button.

One unit of day warehouse supervisor is assigned to work 40 hours on the task. Microsoft Project assumes that the day warehouse supervisor works for the duration of the task if you do not enter a duration in the Work field.

The Task Form looks like the following illustration.

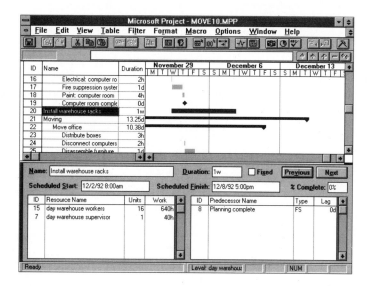

Notice that the duration of the task does not change. Microsoft Project assumes that the additional resource works in parallel with the other resources assigned to the task.

Save your project

Save button

▶   Click the Save button on the tool bar.

Change the resource "driving" the task's duration

You need to increase the day warehouse supervisor's hours because the supervisor needs to spend eight extra hours organizing materials and planning during the rack installation.

1   Select the Work field for day warehouse supervisor.

2   Type **48h**

3   Choose the OK button.

The task duration increases from one week (1w) to 1.2 weeks (1.2w). Note that the work for the day warehouse workers is still 640 hours.

Because the work per unit for the day warehouse workers is 40 hours, while the work per unit for the day warehouse supervisor is now 48 hours, the day warehouse supervisor resource is "driving" the task duration. Increasing the number of day warehouse workers does not shorten the task duration, but increasing the number of day warehouse supervisors does.

4   In the Units field for day warehouse workers, type **12**

5   Choose the OK button.

Now the day warehouse workers resource drives the task duration. Because you decreased the number of day warehouse workers, the work per unit is now more than 48 hours.

The duration changes to 1.33w because the day warehouse workers are now driving the task.

The Task Form looks like the following illustration.

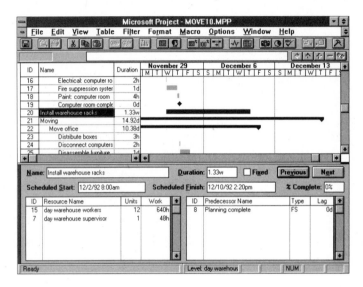

Using Fixed-Duration Tasks

You may prefer to use the fixed-duration scheduling method for certain tasks—especially when you expect a task to take a certain amount of time to complete regardless of assigned resources.

Designate a task as fixed-duration

You want to allow everyone one week for the "Review at corporate level" task, because each reviewer reads the project proposal independently. Designate this task as fixed-duration so you can add reviewers without changing the duration.

1   In the Gantt Chart, select task 4, "Review at corporate level."

2   In the Task Form, select the Fixed check box.

3   Choose the OK button.

Now the duration for this task is one week, no matter how many people review the project proposal.

Add resources to a fixed-duration task

Originally, when the resource for this task was entered, there was only one vice president. However, Victory Sports has just completed reorganizing the rapidly growing groups, so there are now three vice presidents, all of whom want to review your proposal. Increase the number of reviewers for the "Review at corporate level" task.

1   In the Task Form, select the Units field for vice president.

2   Type **3**

3   Choose the OK button.

> Note that the duration is still one week but that the work has increased from 40 hours to 120 hours. No matter how many people review the project proposal, each needs one week to finish the job.

The Task Form looks like the following illustration.

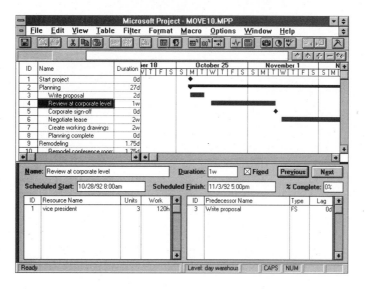

Save button

Save your project

▶   Click the Save button on the tool bar.

One Step Further

You can set the default scheduling method for tasks by choosing the Preferences command from the Options menu and selecting Fixed or Not Fixed for the Default Duration Type setting.

It's best to choose your default scheduling method before you enter tasks, because a new default setting doesn't change tasks that you've already entered.

Change the default scheduling method, which is currently resource-driven.

1 From the Options menu, choose Preferences.

The Preferences dialog box contains options (on the left) with settings (on the right).

2 Click the Default Duration Type option.

The current setting is Not Fixed.

3 Select Fixed from the entry bar list.

If you choose the OK button and later enter new tasks, they default to the fixed-duration setting.

Keep in mind that you can change the scheduling method for a group of selected tasks all at once by selecting them, clicking the Form button on the tool bar, and then selecting the Fixed check box.

4 Since you don't need this for future exercises, choose the Cancel button to close the dialog box and cancel the changes.

If You Want to Continue to the Next Lesson

Save and close your project file

1 From the File menu, choose Close.

2 Choose the Yes button if you see the message box asking whether you want to save your work.

If You Want to Quit Microsoft Project for Now

Save and quit Microsoft Project

1 From the File menu, choose Exit.

2 Choose the Yes button if you see the message box asking whether you want to save your work.

Lesson Summary

To	Do this
Use resource-driven scheduling	This is the default scheduling method. You do not need to make any special selections. As you add resources to a resource-driven task, its duration decreases.
Use fixed-duration scheduling	Click the Fixed check box in the Task Form.

For more information, see in the *Microsoft Project User's Reference*

Scheduling Methods   448

For an online lesson, see in the Microsoft Project for Windows Online Tutorial

Adjusting Schedules

Entering Resources

Preview of the Next Lesson

In the next lesson, you'll learn how to use different views and filters to examine and identify resource allocations. You will learn a variety of ways to resolve resource conflicts. In addition, you'll set a baseline for the project, so that in later lessons you can compare your current schedule with original plan information.

Managing Resource Workloads

In this lesson, you'll learn about ways you can manage overallocated resources to resolve resource conflicts. You'll adjust resource workloads and learn to identify and resolve delays caused by resource problems.

You will learn how to:

- View resource workloads.
- Identify overallocated resources.
- Resolve resource conflicts.
- Set a baseline for the project.

Estimated lesson time: 30 minutes

Start Microsoft Project

If you closed Microsoft Project in the last lesson, you need to restart the application before you can continue.

▶ Double-click the Microsoft Project icon.

Start the lesson

Follow these steps to open the project file called PRACT11.MPP and rename it MOVE11.MPP.

1 From the File menu, choose Open.

2 In the Directories box, double-click PRACTICE.

3 In the File Name box, double-click PRACT11.MPP.

4 From the File menu, choose Save As.

5 In the File Name box, type **MOVE11.MPP**

6 Choose the OK button.

Microsoft Project stores your project on your hard disk with the filename MOVE11.MPP.

Resolving Resource Conflicts

When you first open the project for this lesson, you see the Resource Sheet. This form provides an overview of all the resources used in the project. In this lesson, you learn to use other helpful tools for viewing how resources are allocated in your project.

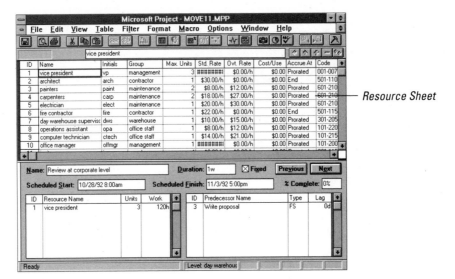

— *Resource Sheet*

Resource conflicts occur when the amount of a particular resource required at a given time exceeds the specified maximum units for that resource. For example, you might have two painters assigned to paint the conference room at the same time three painters are scheduled to paint the executive offices. Even though you might have a maximum of four painters available, you need *five* painters to complete both tasks on time. You have a resource allocation conflict because the number of painters you need at a given time exceeds the maximum number of painters available for the project.

Microsoft Project displays a message in the status bar when it finds a resource conflict. Although you can continue to work on your plan, you need to *level* the resources so that your plan accurately reflects the resources required to complete all the tasks. Leveling resources means making sure that peak usage of a particular resource never exceeds the maximum number of available units for that resource.

For example, in the case of the overallocated painters, you need to make adjustments to the plan so that you never need more than four painters at one time, or else you would need to increase the number of painters on the project team. Microsoft Project offers several ways to resolve a resource conflict.

- You can choose to level resources manually if your project requires using several strategies to level resources. Leveling resources yourself allows you to try a variety of other adjustments to resource assignments or to task schedules according to the specific needs in your project.

- You can use resource leveling commands to have Microsoft Project resolve resource conflicts for you. These commands resolve the conflict by delaying overlapping tasks which caused the conflict. If you used the commands, Microsoft Project would resolve the resource conflict with the painters, mentioned above, by rescheduling the start of painting the executive offices after painting the conference room had been completed.

- You can also enlist the aid of *PlanningWizards*, which are built-in "helpers" that guide you in the use of several Microsoft Project operations, including the process of leveling resources. PlanningWizards are particularly helpful if you are familiar with the general process and concepts, but need a "hint" about specific steps. You can learn about the different PlanningWizards by selecting the PlanningWizards command on the Help menu. From the PlanningWizards menu, you can select "What are PlanningWizards?" to get an overview of the operations for which they are available. At the end of this lesson, the section called "One Step Further" guides you in using a PlanningWizard to level resources.

Resolving Resource Conflicts Yourself

When you need to resolve the conflict yourself, you can use any one or a combination of the following strategies. The steps in this lesson help you discover for yourself the different alternatives you might try in your own projects.

Increase the maximum units of a resource available   Enter a larger number of maximum units in the Resource Form or on the Resource Sheet.

Assign a different resource to the overallocated task   Determine if you have another comparable resource available that could do the work. For example, assigning the operations assistant to a task might free the operations manager for another task. You can do this in any view in which you can assign resources to tasks.

Adjust task relationships or constraints   When two overlapping tasks cause an allocation conflict, you may be able to reschedule a task so that one task starts later.

Allow overtime   You can enter overtime work for the resource in the Ovt Work field in the Task Form or in the Resource Form. Overtime work is paid at the overtime rate.

Extend working days and hours on the resource calendar   Use this method (instead of entering overtime work) if you don't want the additional work to be incurred at the overtime rate, and you want the additional work to be included in the task schedule.

Using Resource Management Tools

After you finish assigning resources, you can review resource workloads to make sure you're using resources efficiently. Among the many resource management tools available in Microsoft Project are the Resource Usage view, the Resource Allocation view, the Overallocated filter, and the Resource Graph. Start by displaying the Resource Usage view to see when and to what extent each resource is being used.

Display the Resource Usage view

The Resource Usage view displays resource usage over time in a table format. Use this view to determine to what extent a resource is overused or underused. By locating underallocated resources you can identify resources that can assist or replace overallocated resources.

1 Move to the top view.

2 From the View menu, choose Resource Usage.

The Resource Usage view appears, displaying a list of resources and a timescale that shows allocations.

3 Scroll to the beginning of the project.

You can also use ALT+HOME to move quickly to the beginning.

Your Resource Usage view looks like the following illustration.

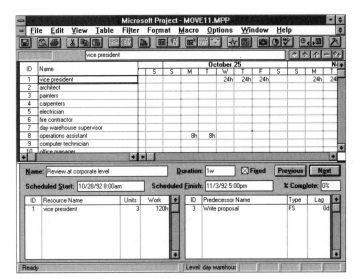

Change the units on the timescale to months and weeks

The timescale now shows only a portion of the project. You want to be sure that resources are not overallocated at any point during the project. Change the units on the timescale to show a greater time span.

Zoom Out button

▶ Click the Timescale Zoom Out button on the tool bar twice.

Your view looks like the following illustration.

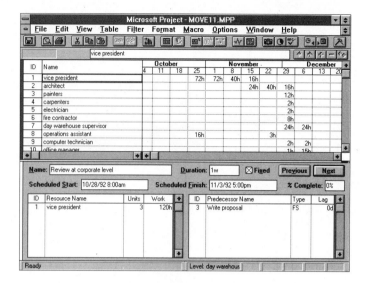

Apply the Overallocated filter to Resource Usage

Overallocated resources are displayed in red on a color monitor or in bold on a monochrome monitor. If you want to see only the overallocated resources, you can apply the Overallocated filter.

1 From the Filter menu, choose Overallocated.

Resource 15, day warehouse workers, is shown as the overallocated resource.

2 From the Filter menu, choose All Resources to display all resources again.

Display the Resource Graph

The *Resource Graph* provides a graphical representation of resource usage over time. Use the Resource Graph to see a profile of a resource's allocation, work, and cost. This view helps you see when you have more units assigned than are available, as specified in the maximum units field on the Task Form. You can view information for an individual resource, a group of resources, or both.

In the following steps, you first go to the field containing the overallocated day warehouse workers. Then you display the Resource Graph in the bottom view to get a graphical representation of peak units for this resource.

1 From the Edit menu, choose Go To.

You can also press F5 to open the Go To dialog box.

2 In the ID box, type **15**

3 Choose the OK button.

4 Click the Task Form.

You can also press F6 to switch between views.

5   From the View menu, choose Resource Graph.

The Resource Graph shows that, during the weeks of November 29 and December 6, the peak usage for day warehouse workers is 22 but the maximum number of workers available is 15. (The maximum number of workers is specified in the Maximum Units field in the Resource Edit Form and displayed on the Resource Graph.) The day warehouse workers resource is overallocated by 7 units.

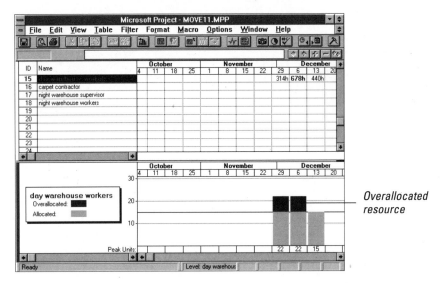

View Task Assignments

To find out which tasks the overallocated day warehouse workers are assigned to, use the Resource Allocation view. This view consists of the Resource Usage view over the Delay Gantt view. It does not appear on the View menu, but you can display it using the Define Views command.

1   From the View menu, choose Define Views.

2   In the Views box, select Resource Allocation.

3   Choose the Set button to display the view.

     The Delay Gantt view shows all the tasks to which the day warehouse workers are assigned. Note that the "Install warehouse racks" and "Move office furniture/ boxes" tasks overlap, which is when the peak usage occurs.

Even though task 25 overlaps with task 20 on November 29, the total number of workers required is only 14, so task 25 does not result in an overallocated resource conflict.

Your view looks like the following illustration.

Peak usage

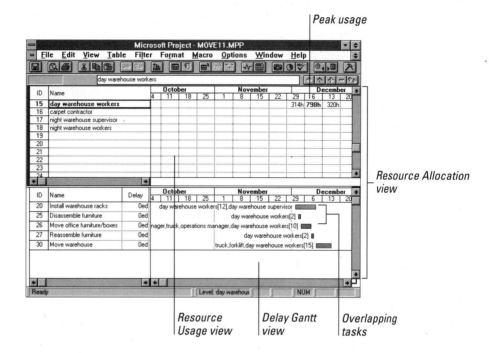

Resource Allocation view

Resource Usage view

Delay Gantt view

Overlapping tasks

Substitute a resource

You can see in the Resource Usage view that the night warehouse workers are not assigned to any move tasks during the period when the day warehouse workers are overallocated. First find out how many day warehouse workers are assigned to the "Move office furniture/boxes" task. Next replace the day warehouse workers with the night warehouse workers for this task.

Resource Assignment button

1   In the Delay Gantt view, select task 26, "Move office furniture/boxes."

2   Click the Resource Assignment button on the tool bar.

3   In the Resources box, select day warehouse workers from the list.

4   Choose the Replace button.

5   In the With box, select **night warehouse workers** from the list.

6   With the insertion point at the end of the line, type **[10]**

You need to assign 10 night warehouse workers.

7   Choose the OK button.

The message "Level: day warehouse workers" is no longer displayed in the status bar.

By assigning a different, equally capable resource to move the furniture and boxes, you have solved the overallocation problems for the day warehouse workers.

Leveling Resources Automatically

If the best solution for leveling resources is to delay overlapping tasks (tasks that occur at the same time), you can have Microsoft Project resolve resource conflicts for you by using the Leveling and Level Now commands on the Options menu. With the Leveling command, you can have Microsoft Project level the resource as soon as it becomes overallocated. Or, if you prefer, you can elect to have Microsoft Project level only when you choose the Level Now command.

When Microsoft Project levels a resource, it adds a delay in the Delay field in the Delay Gantt view for the task (except for tasks already in progress). You use the Delay Gantt view to display Gantt bars that show delay and *slack* (the amount of time between the end of one task and the start of its successor) to see how Microsoft Project delayed each overallocated task. If an individual delay is not what you want, you can choose to remove the delay. You can also choose Undo Level from the Edit menu immediately after leveling to remove all changes.

Creating a Baseline

Now that you have resolved the resource conflict in the schedule, the current plan represents your best estimate of how the project should proceed and what resources it will take to accomplish the move. Therefore, you can now save your project information as a baseline for future comparisons to actual progress. The Set Plan command on the Options menu stores a copy of task and resource information. The information is "frozen" and is used for reference purposes only.

Microsoft Project uses this data to calculate and display *variance*—the difference between what was originally planned and what is currently scheduled.

Create a baseline for future comparisons

Set the plan for the project as your baseline. In later lessons, you'll compare this data to updated project information.

1   From the <u>V</u>iew menu, choose Task <u>E</u>ntry.

2   From the <u>O</u>ptions menu, choose Se<u>t</u> Plan.

The options selected in the dialog box are all correct for setting the plan, so you don't need to change them. In Lesson 14, "Tracking Project Progress," you learn more about the different options available when setting the plan.

3   Choose the OK button.

One Step Further

If you decide to delay overlapping tasks to resolve the resource conflict, you can choose to have Microsoft Project resolve the conflict for you. To help you learn how to use this feature, you can use the PlanningWizard that is available for resolving resource conflicts. This PlanningWizard guides you through the process of selecting resources and choosing the correct commands to have Microsoft Project level resources for you.

In these steps, you use the same project file you opened at the start of this lesson.

1 Open PRACT11.MPP and save it with the new name **MOVE11A.MPP**.

2 From the Help menu, choose PlanningWizards.

3 On the PlanningWizard menu, click the Resolving Resource Conflicts option button and choose the Next button.

The next five Wizard messages explain the parts of the Resource Allocation view and provide an overview of the process of resolving conflicts. After you read each Wizard message, choose the Next button to continue.

4 When the PlanningWizard displays the message to choose the resource you want to level, scroll to resource ID 15 "day warehouse workers" and select it. Choose the Next button.

5 When the PlanningWizard prompts you to look for another overallocated resource, click the Overallocation button on the tool bar. Read the next Wizard message and choose the Next button to continue.

6 When you see the menu of leveling options, click option button 4, "Have Microsoft Project Level;" choose the Next button to continue.

7 Because there are no more resources to level, choose the Next button to continue. Read the next Wizard message and choose the Next button to continue.

8 Follow the PlanningWizard instructions to choose the Leveling command from the Options menu. In the Leveling dialog box, make sure the Manual option is selected, the "Delay Only Within Slack" check box is cleared, and the "Automatically Remove Delay" check box is checked. Then choose the Next button to continue.

9 Follow the PlanningWizard instructions to choose the Level Now command from the Options menu. Make sure the Selection option button is selected. Click OK in the Level Now dialog box.

10 After the PlanningWizard informs you that the resource conflict is resolved, choose the Stop button to return to your project.

11 From the Options menu, choose Project Status and note that the Scheduled Finish date for the project is now 12/23/92.

When you levelled resources manually by substituting a resource, your project finished on 12/17/92. Having Microsoft Project resolve the resource conflict by adding delays extended project completion by six days.

If You Want to Continue to the Next Lesson

Save and close your project file

1   From the File menu, choose Close.

2   Choose the Yes button if you see the message box asking whether you want to save your work.

If You Want to Quit Microsoft Project for Now

Save and quit Microsoft Project

1   From the File menu, choose Exit.

2   Choose the Yes button if you see the message box asking whether you want to save your work.

Lesson Summary

To	Do this
View resource workloads	Choose the Resource Graph or Resource Usage views on the View menu. Choose Define Views from the View menu, and choose Resource Allocation.
Resolve resource conflicts	Resolve the conflicts yourself by adjusting individual resource assignments and task schedules.
	Or choose the Leveling and Level now commands on the Options menu to have Microsoft Project add delays to overlapping tasks assigned to overallocated resources.
	Or choose the PlanningWizards to step you through the process.
Set a baseline for the project	Use the Set Plan command on the Options menu.

For more information, see in the *Microsoft Project User's Reference*

Leveling Resources   212

Resource Graph   403

Resource Usage View   423

For an online lesson, see in the Microsoft Project for Windows Online Tutorial

Managing Resources

Preview of the Next Lesson

In the next lesson, you will learn how to determine whether tasks are over budget. You also will learn about different strategies for reducing costs to meet the budget.

Review & Practice

In the lessons in Part 3, "Working with Resources," you learned skills to help you enter and schedule resource information in a project. If you want to practice these skills and test your knowledge before you proceed with the lessons in Part 4, you can work through the Review & Practice section following this lesson.

Part 3   Review & Practice

Before you begin planning a project of your own, practice the skills you learned in Part 3 by working through the project management activities in this Review & Practice section. You'll define the people, equipment, and materials needed to prepare the annual report for Victory Sports. You will assign resources to the tasks you entered in the project from the Part 2 Review & Practice . You'll also set up a resource calendar to define a resource's availability, check resource usage, resolve overallocations, and obtain cost estimates to complete specific tasks.

Scenario

As project manager for the annual report, you have obtained help with the production of the annual report. People from your department and others will be involved. You will also have outside resources to complete specialized tasks. In your role as project manager, you need to track who will do each task, when they will do it, and when they are available.

You will review and practice how to:

- Enter resources.

- Change calendars.

- Resolve resource overallocations.

- Analyze cost information.

Estimated practice time: 30 minutes

Before You Begin

1   Open the scenario project called 3ANNUAL.MPP.

2   Save the project file as ANNUAL3.MPP.

This project file should look similar to the file you saved after completing the steps in the Part 2 Review & Practice. However, notice that some tasks already have some resources assigned and that several resources are already defined in the resource pool.

Step 1: Enter Resources

Use the Resource Sheet view to add the following resource information in the resource pool:

- Office temps at $15/hour; you have approval to hire two temporaries. Use TMP for the initials.

- Intern at $10/hour; there is only one intern. Use INT for the initials.

For more information on	See
Entering resources	Lesson 8

Step 2: Assign Resources to Tasks

Return to the Task Entry View, then use the Resource Assignment button on the tool bar to assign these resources to these tasks. The number in brackets [ ] is the number of individuals assigned to the task.

Resource	Task ID
Office temp [1]	30, 33
Intern	11, 12, 13, 18
Office temp [1]	18, 24, 26

For more information on	See
Assigning resources to tasks	Lesson 8

Step 3: Change the Calendar

Make a New Base Calendar

Create a copy of the Standard base calendar, and call it Summer. Specify a holiday and indicate a half-day schedule on Mondays. Be sure to save your calendar by choosing the Save button in the Base Calendars dialog box. Assign this calendar as the base calendar for the schedule by selecting it from the Calendar drop down list in the Project Info dialog box.

The first Monday in September: National holiday.

Monday Start time: 1:00 P.M. Finish time: 5:00 P.M.

For more information on	See
Changing the Standard calendar	Lesson 9

Modify a Resource Calendar

Change the calendar for the intern to reflect the fact that the intern does not work on the third Friday in August.

For more information on	See
Making new calendars	Lesson 9

Step 4: Schedule Resources

Specify that the duration for task 17 is not affected by the number of vice presidents assigned to the task. The Task Form indicates that this is a fixed-duration task. It also indicates that senior managers will be involved in the reviews.

For more information on	See
Scheduling with resources	Lesson 10

Step 5: Review Resource Workloads

Use the Resource Usage view and Resource Graph to display resource workloads over time.

For more information on	See
Scheduling with resources	Lesson 11

Step 6: Level Resource Workloads

Resolve overallocated resource conflicts for the writers. Use the Leveling command with the Manual option to have Microsoft Project level the resources for you. When you are ready to level resources, choose the Level Now command.

Notice how Microsoft Project eliminates overallocations by delaying tasks.

For more information on	See
Resolving resource conflicts	Lesson 11

Save button

Return to the Task Entry view and save your project

1 From the <u>V</u>iew menu, choose Task <u>E</u>ntry.

2 Click the Save button on the tool bar.

If You Want to Continue to the Next Lesson

Close your project file

▶ From the <u>F</u>ile menu, choose <u>C</u>lose.

If You Want to Quit Microsoft Project for Now

Quit Microsoft Project

▶ From the <u>F</u>ile menu, choose E<u>x</u>it.

Adjusting Project Costs

In this lesson, you'll learn how to identify tasks that are over budget and how to use different strategies for reducing costs to meet your original planned expenditures. If detailed cost management is not one of your usual project responsibilities, feel free to skip this lesson for now, and return to it later when you need to become familiar with cost management concepts.

In this lesson you learn how to:

- Change the current date.
- Identify tasks that are over budget.
- Reduce costs to meet the budget.

Estimated lesson time: 25 minutes

Start Microsoft Project

If you closed Microsoft Project in the last lesson, you need to restart the application before you can continue.

▶ Double-click the Microsoft Project icon.

Start the lesson

Do the following to open the project file called PRACT12.MPP and rename it MOVE12.MPP.

1 From the File menu, choose Open.

2 In the Directories box, double-click PRACTICE.

3 In the File Name box, double-click PRACT12.MPP.

4 From the File menu, choose Save As.

5 In the File Name box, type **MOVE12.MPP**

6 Choose the OK button.

   Microsoft Project stores your project on your hard disk with the filename MOVE12.MPP.

7 Press ALT+HOME to set the timescale at the beginning of the project.

Change the current date

The following steps set the current date in Microsoft Project to reflect the passage of time to just before the project is scheduled to begin. With new information you have determined since you set the plan, you can update the schedule and compare this information with what you planned originally.

1   From the Options menu, choose Project Info.

2   In the Current Date box, type **10/5/92 10:00 am**

3   Choose the OK button.

4   Scroll to the week of October 4.

Notice the date line moved to October 5.

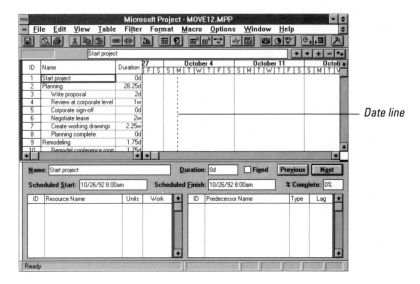

— *Date line*

Computing Costs

The cost of a task is the sum of the fixed cost plus the cost of its resource assignments. The resource cost is calculated from the resource unit cost information—standard rate, overtime rate, cost per use, and accrual method—you enter for the resource.

For example, a task with one resource that is assigned to do 40 hours of work at a standard rate of $10 per hour has a resource cost of $400. A task with two resources assigned, each incurring a cost of $400, has a resource cost of $800. You view the resource costs in the Cost table.

Comparing Costs Using the Cost Table

The Cost table displays columns of cost information that make it easy to compare scheduled, planned, and actual costs. Apply the Cost table in a resource view to see resource costs. To see task costs, you apply the Cost table in a task view.

View the current budget

It is now October 5, and the project start is only three weeks away. You set your plan on July 20, but since then you updated work estimates on a few of the corporate move tasks. You updated your project schedule with the new information and want to see how the changes have affected the cost of the move.

A quick way to check the overall budget is to use the Project Status command. Check to see how the current estimate compares to the budget by comparing the scheduled cost to the planned cost.

Project Status button

1   Click the Project Status button on the tool bar.

A Project Status report appears. In the Cost column, you can see that the scheduled cost is somewhat more than the planned cost.

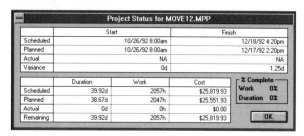

Project Status for MOVE12.MPP		
	Start	Finish
Scheduled	10/26/92 8:00am	12/18/92 4:20pm
Planned	10/26/92 8:00am	12/17/92 2:20pm
Actual	NA	NA
Variance	0d	1.25d

	Duration	Work	Cost	% Complete
Scheduled	39.92d	2057h	$25,819.93	Work 0%
Planned	38.67d	2047h	$25,551.93	Duration 0%
Actual	0d	0h	$0.00	
Remaining	39.92d	2057h	$25,819.93	OK

2   Choose the OK button.

View task cost information with the Cost table

To find a way to lower the project costs, look at the costs for individual tasks. Display the Task Sheet in the top view and apply the Cost table.

1   From the View menu, choose Task Sheet.

2   From the Table menu, choose Cost.

Your screen looks like the following illustration.

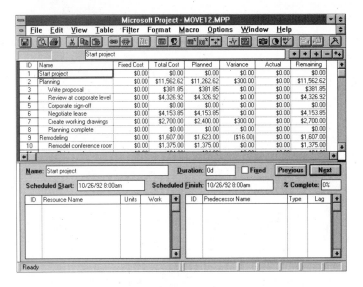

Reducing Costs

You can use filters supplied with Microsoft Project to focus on tasks and resources that exceed the budget. The *Overbudget filter*, available in task views, displays tasks whose scheduled costs exceed planned costs. The *Cost Overbudget filter*, available in resource views, displays resources whose scheduled costs exceed planned costs. You can reduce task costs in many ways. Use the filters to identify the method that is best for your project.

Substitute higher-cost, more efficient resources   For example, an experienced engineer might cost more, but may work much faster than a less-experienced engineer. Because a more efficient resource works fewer hours on a task, you can pay a higher rate and still reduce the cost of the resource assignment.

Trade equipment expenses for labor costs   If adding equipment lets your employees work faster, you may save more in labor than you spend on the extra equipment. For example, if you are renting only one scaffold, you might consider renting a second to speed the task.

Substitute a lower-cost resource   As illustrated in the following steps, another way to reduce costs is to assign a less-expensive, but equally effective resource. For example, a $150-per-day draftsman might be able to do some of a $250-per-day architect's work.

Display the tasks that are over budget

You want to focus on tasks that are over budget. Applying the Overbudget filter is a quick way to find out which tasks exceed the budget. After viewing only the over budget tasks, set the view to display all tasks.

1 From the Filter menu, choose Overbudget.

The "Create working drawings" task is the only task that is over budget. The "Planning" phase is over budget because the "Create working drawings" task under it is over budget. The Variance field shows that the task is over budget by $300.

2 From the Filter menu, choose All Tasks.

Examine resource assignments

You need to find out why the costs for the task have increased before you can find a way to lower the costs. Use the resource work information on the Task Form to examine the work assignment for this task.

1 Select task 7, "Create working drawings."

The Task Form displays information about the task's resource assignments and predecessors.

2 Move to the Task Form.

3 From the Format menu, choose Resource Work.

The bottom of the Task Form shows the work fields for the architect.

You can see in the Work field that the work estimate for the architect increased from the planned work of 80 hours to the currently scheduled work of 90 hours.

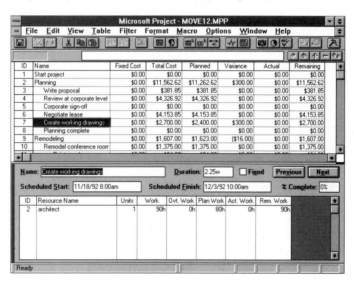

Transfer work to a new, less expensive resource

Since the original estimate was made for the "Create working drawings" task, an additional draftsman has been hired to do some of the work on the task. The draftsman's standard rate is $20 per hour as opposed to the architect's standard rate of $30 per hour. Add the draftsman to the task and transfer 30 hours of work to the draftsman.

1   In the Task Form, select the blank Resource Name field below architect.

2   Type **draftsman**

3   In the Work field for the draftsman, type **30h**

4   In the Work field for the architect, type **60h**

5   Choose the OK button.

A message appears asking if you want to add the resource draftsman to the resource pool.

6   Choose the Yes button.

The Resource Edit Form dialog box appears.

Enter the resource information for the draftsman

1   Select the Initials box.

2   In the Initials box, drag across the default initial "d" to select it.

You can also press TAB.

3   Type **draft**

4   Select the Std Rate box and type **$20/h**

5   In the Accrue At box, select End.

Both the architect and the draftsman are paid upon completion of the work so the cost does not accrue until the end of a task.

6   In the Group box, type **contractor**

7   In the Code box, type **501-110**

This code is the Victory Sports accounting code for this kind of contractor.

8   Choose the OK button.

Microsoft Project recalculates the cost of the resources for this task.

The cost for the task is once again $2,400, so your project is back within budget. The Variance field for the "Create working drawings" task contains 0 (zero) because the scheduled cost and the planned cost are the same.

9   From the View menu, choose Task Entry.

10   Click anywhere in the Task Form to make it active.

11   From the Format menu, choose Resources & Predecessors.

Save button

Save your project

▶   Click the Save button on the tool bar.

One Step Further

An "underbudget" filter can be used to locate extra funds in case other tasks are over budget. Follow these steps to create and apply a filter that looks for tasks that are under budget. Click in the Task Sheet in the top view to make it active before you begin.

1   From the Filter menu, choose Define Filters.

2   Choose the New button.

3   In the Name field, type **Underbudget**

4   In the Field Name column, use the down arrow in the entry bar to select Cost Variance.

5   In the Test column, use the down arrow in the entry bar to select Less.

6   In the Value(s) column, type **0**

7   Choose the OK button.

8   Choose the Set button to apply the new filter.

After viewing only the under budget tasks, reset the view to display all tasks.

9   From the Filter menu, choose All Tasks.

If You Want to Continue to the Next Lesson

Save and close your project file

1   From the File menu, choose Close.

2   Choose the Yes button if you see the message box asking whether you want to save your work.

If You Want to Quit Microsoft Project for Now

Save and quit Microsoft Project

1   From the File menu, choose Exit.

2   Choose the Yes button if you see the message box asking whether you want to save your work.

Lesson Summary

To	Do this
Identify tasks that are over budget	Choose the Task Sheet view from the View menu. Next, choose the Cost table from the Table menu, then choose the Overbudget filter from the Filter menu.
Reduce costs to meet the budget	From within the Task Form, choose Resource Work from the Format menu. Examine resource assignments, and determine if you should substitute lower-cost equally effective rresources; substitute higher- cost, more efficient resources; or add equipment to reduce labor time.

For more information, see in the *Microsoft Project User's Reference*

Costs   44

Tracking Progress   567

For an online lesson, see in the Microsoft Project for Windows Online Tutorial

Entering Resources

Preview of the Next Lesson

In the next lesson, "Managing the Schedule," you will specify constraints for task start and finish dates. You will also learn how to track the progress of the project after it has started, and how to shorten the project schedule by shortening the critical path.

Scheduling Task Constraints

In this lesson, you'll learn to apply task contraints to restrict how Microsoft Project schedules tasks. You'll also learn how to resolve scheduling conflicts that may result when you apply task constraints in the schedule.

You will learn how to:

- Use constraints to set time limitations.
- Resolve constraint conflicts.

Estimated lesson time: 30 minutes

Start Microsoft Project

If you closed Microsoft Project in the last lesson, you need to restart the application before you can continue.

▶ Double-click the Microsoft Project icon.

Start the lesson

Do the following to open the project file called PRACT13.MPP and rename it MOVE13.MPP.

1 From the File menu, choose Open.

2 In the Directories box, double-click PRACTICE.

3 In the File Name box, double-click PRACT13.MPP.

4 From the File menu, choose Save As.

5 In the File Name box, type **MOVE13.MPP**

6 Choose the OK button.

   Microsoft Project stores your project on your hard disk with the filename MOVE13.MPP.

7 Press ALT+HOME to set the timescale at the beginning of the project.

Applying Task Constraints

Constraints are schedule restrictions that you place on individual tasks to affect task start and finish dates. Constraints can be general, as in As Soon As Possible, or very specific, as in Must Finish On November 12. With such constraints applied to tasks, Microsoft Project creates a project schedule that meets the realities of your project.

Use the Constraint box in the Task Edit Form dialog box to set constraints for individual tasks or groups of tasks.

You can apply any one of these eight constraints to individual tasks:

- As Late As Possible
- As Soon As Possible
- Finish No Earlier Than
- Finish No Later Than
- Must Finish On
- Must Start On
- Start No Earlier Than
- Start No Later Than

The default task constraint is As Soon As Possible.

Constraint Dates

All constraints (except As Soon As Possible and As Late As Possible) are based on a date you specify. Constraint dates tie tasks to specific calendar dates. Use constraint dates to reflect deadlines and availability of resources. For example, you can schedule the painting tasks to Start No Earlier Than November 26, the date the paint arrives. Constraint dates do not vary with other changes in the schedule; rather, the constraint is used in scheduling the other dates in the plan.

Resolving Constraint Conflicts

Constraints can affect the project finish date or conflict with other scheduling requirements. If there is a conflict, Microsoft Project displays a message. To get more information about how to resolve the conflict, click the Help button in the message box. In this lesson, you'll learn to resolve scheduling conflicts by adjusting task dates, relationships, or constraints.

Schedule tasks as late as possible

The computers and office furniture are essential to the operation of Victory Sports. Schedule the tasks "Disconnect computers" and "Disassemble furniture" to start as late as possible without delaying any other tasks. Use the Multiple Task Edit Form dialog box to schedule the tasks as late as possible.

1   Select task 24, "Disconnect computers," and task 25, "Disassemble furniture."

2   Scroll the Gantt Chart to the week of November 29, 1992.

Form button

3   Click the Form button on the tool bar to open the Multiple Task Edit Form dialog box.

4   In the Constraint box, click the arrow under Constraint to display the list.

5   Select As Late As Possible from the Constraint list.

You don't need to enter a date for the As Soon As Possible or the As Late As Possible constraints, as they aren't tied to a certain day. Watch the Gantt bars for these tasks as you do the next step. If the dialog box is covering the Gantt bars for these tasks, drag the dialog box title bar to move it away from the Gantt bars.

6   Choose the OK button.

The tasks shift within their slack to the latest possible start dates.

Your Gantt Chart looks like the following illustration.

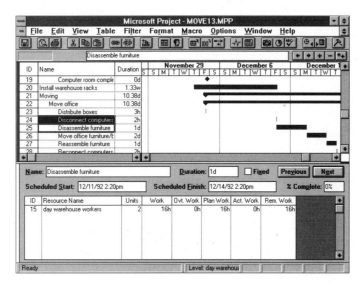

Level overallocated resources

Now that "Disconnect computers" and "Disassemble furniture" start as late as possible, the day warehouse workers are overallocated again. The message "Level: day warehouse workers" appears at the bottom of your screen.

Adding more day warehouse workers can solve the problem. Fortunately, two new day warehouse workers were hired recently. Add them to the resources available, bringing the total to 17.

1 From the View menu, choose Resource Sheet.

2 In the Max. Units field for day warehouse workers, type **17**

3 Click the enter box on the entry bar or press ENTER.

Now the tasks "Disconnect computers" and "Disassemble furniture" can start as late as possible, with no overallocation for day warehouse workers.

Schedule tasks to finish before a date

The president has arranged for a sports personality to come to Victory Sports to endorse a new product on December 14. Marketing wants to use the conference room for the event. Schedule the milestone "Conference room complete" to finish no later than December 7. This allows one week to correct any problems before the publicity session is held.

1 From the View menu, choose Gantt Chart.

2 Double-click task 14, "Conference room complete."

The Task Edit Form dialog box appears. Another way to display the Task Edit Form dialog box is to double-click a task.

3 In the Task Edit Form dialog box, click the arrow under Constraint to display the list.

4 Select Finish No Later Than from the list.

5 In the Date box, type **12/7/92**

The task is scheduled to finish no later than December 7.

6 Choose the OK button.

The milestone "Conference room complete" is not affected by this constraint because it is already scheduled to finish before December 7. This constraint ensures that future scheduling changes do not cause the task to finish beyond December 7.

Schedule tasks to start after a set date

Your first choice of carpeting isn't going to be in stock until December 14. The carpet contractor wants to know if he should place the order or substitute your second choice which is available right away. What effect does this new constraint have on the schedule? Enter the constraint Start No Earlier Than December 14 for task 12, "Lay carpet: conference room."

1 Double-click task 12, "Lay carpet: conference room," to display the Task Edit Form dialog box.

2 In the Constraint box, select Start No Earlier Than from the list.

3 In the Date box, type **12/14/92**

4 Choose the OK button.

Microsoft Project displays a message that a task has a scheduling conflict.

Because you just put a constraint on when the room had to be ready, Microsoft Project won't allow you to make this change. If you cannot start to lay the carpet before December 14, other tasks cannot be completed on schedule.

Display the Help message

Microsoft Project Help gives you a more detailed message about the conflict.

1 Choose the Help button to display Help about the message.

You can also press F1.

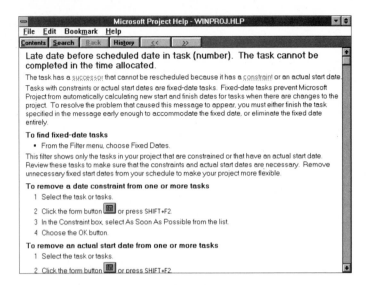

To summarize, the Help window explains that the predecessor task must be completed early enough to accommodate a fixed-date successor (task 14, "Conference room complete"), or you must remove the fixed-date constraint in the predecessor task to correct the conflict.

2   Choose Exit from the File menu in the Help window to close it.

3   Choose the OK button.

Examine the conflict

Because task 14 marks the end of the conference room remodeling phase, look for any task relationships, dates, or other constraints that can be changed in task 14, or its predecessors, to eliminate the conflict. Use the Task Details Form command to get additional details for each task including constraint information.

1   In the Gantt Chart, select task 14, "Conference room complete."

2   Move to the Task Form.

3   From the View menu, choose Define Views.

4   In the Views box, select Task Details Form.

5   Choose the Set button to display the view.

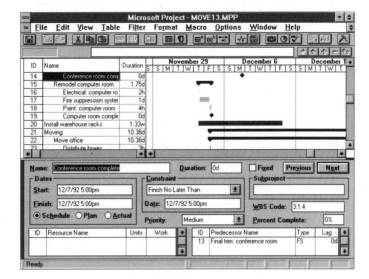

The Task Details Form displays the constraint as "Finish No Later Than December 7." The finish of the conference room cannot be changed because of the upcoming new product announcement.

The Task Details Form also lists the predecessor "Final trim: conference room" and the relationship to the task.

6   Choose the Previous button to view task 13, "Final trim: conference room."

The constraint is As Soon As Possible. Task 12, "Lay carpet: conference room," must precede this task.

No other scheduling restrictions are evident, so no changes can be made to this task to correct the conflict. You must tell the carpet contractor to install your second choice of carpeting.

Correct the conflict

To proceed with this exercise you must correct the conflict. Until you correct a scheduling conflict, Microsoft Project continues to display warning messages each time you make a change to your schedule. Do the following to remove the constraint from task 12, "Lay carpet: conference room."

1   In the Gantt Chart, double-click task 12, "Lay carpet: conference room."

2   In the Constraint box, select As Soon As Possible from the list.

3   Choose the OK button.

The date you entered earlier is removed.

Return to the Task Entry view

1   From the View menu, choose Task Entry.

2   Move to the Task Form.

3   From the Format menu, choose Resources & Predecessors.

Your screen looks like the following illustration.

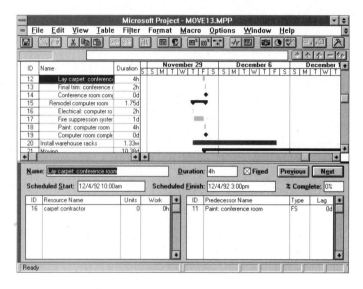

Save button

Save your project

▶   Click the Save button on the tool bar.

One Step Further

You can display all constraints in your project by changing to a Task Sheet view of your task information and applying the Constraint Dates table. Because Microsoft Project can contain many columns of information, tables are a fast way to display a set of useful, related columns.

The Constraint Dates table is also useful when you want to enter the same constraint for a number of tasks.

1   Hold down the SHIFT key and choose Task Sheet from the View menu.

Your screen displays a single-pane view of the Task Sheet.

2   From the Table menu, choose Define Tables.

3   In the Tables box, select Constraint Dates.

4   Choose the Set button to apply the table.

Your screen displays columns containing constraint information for the project. The only task with a constraint date is task 14, "Conference room complete."

Return to the Task Entry view

1   From the Table menu, choose Entry.

2   From the View menu, choose Task Entry.

If You Want to Continue to the Next Lesson

Save and close your project file

1   From the File menu, choose Close.

2   Choose the Yes button if you see the message box asking whether you want to save your work.

If You Want to Quit Microsoft Project for Now

Save and quit Microsoft Project

1   From the File menu, choose Exit.

2   Choose the Yes button if you see the message box asking whether you want to save your work.

Lesson Summary

To	Do this
Set time constraints	In the Task Edit Form, click the down arrow in the Constraint field. Select from the list of constraints the kind of constraint to apply to the selected task.
Examine resource conflicts	From the View menu, choose Define Views, and then select the Task Details Form view.
Resolve constraint conflicts	Add resources to constrained tasks or remove unnecessary predecessors.

For more information, see in the *Microsoft Project User's Reference*

Constraints   37

Task Relationships   535

For an online lesson, see in the Microsoft Project for Windows Online Tutorial

Adjusting Schedules

Preview of the Next Lesson

In the next lesson, you'll learn how to change the schedule to reflect the actual status of the project tasks. You'll learn several ways to indicate when tasks have occurred exactly as planned, experienced delays or slowdowns, or even finished early.

Tracking Project Progress

In this lesson, you'll learn how to track the progress of your project's performance after the project is under way. You will learn to compare the current schedule and actual data to the original.

You will learn how to:

- Update the schedule with actual data.
- Compare the schedule to the plan.
- Compare actual data to the plan.

Estimated lesson time: 30 minutes

Start Microsoft Project

If you closed Microsoft Project in the last lesson, you need to restart the application before you can continue.

▶ Double-click the Microsoft Project icon.

Start the lesson

Do the following to open the project file called PRACT14.MPP and rename it MOVE14.MPP.

1 From the File menu, choose Open.
2 In the Directories box, double-click PRACTICE.
3 In the File Name box, double-click PRACT14.MPP.
4 From the File menu, choose Save As.
5 In the File Name box, type **MOVE14.MPP**
6 Choose the OK button.

   Microsoft Project stores a copy of your project on your hard disk with the filename MOVE14.MPP.

7 Press ALT+HOME to set the timescale at the beginning of the project.

Change today's date and time

Assume it's now December 2, and the office move is well under way. Use the Project Info command to change your current project date to 12/2/92.

1 From the Options menu, choose Project Info.

The Project Information dialog box appears.

2 In the Current Date box, select the date and time and type **12/2/92 10:00am**

3 Choose the OK button.

Tracking Progress

Tracking progress means entering and analyzing your project's performance once the project is under way. Before the project starts, you copy the schedule to a plan. During the project, you compare the current schedule to the original plan. Even with the best plan, the schedule is likely to deviate from the plan. By tracking progress, you can discover which tasks need extra attention in time to make adjustments for your project to continue smoothly.

When tracking progress, you work with three types of information: planned, scheduled, and actual.

Planned   Your fixed model, or baseline, for how the project should go. Plan information (task dates, allocated resources, and budgeted costs) stays the same. For example, you might plan on obtaining waste barrels beginning on October 27, with a duration of two days and a fixed cost of $400. This information is the task's planned data.

Scheduled   A changing, working model for upcoming tasks after the project is under way. The schedule may change as new information is received and actual information is incorporated. For example, before you begin purchasing waste barrels, you might discover you can't begin until October 28 and the barrels will then cost $500. This revised information about the task is the task's scheduled data.

Actual   Tasks already in progress or finished. Actual data is incorporated into the schedule affecting future tasks. After the acquisition of waste barrels is complete, you determine that it took three days to complete. This new information, reflecting the completed task, is the task's actual data.

To track progress, start by using the Set Plan command on the Options menu. This command freezes the data that becomes a baseline against which you can compare your constantly changing schedule. You already created a baseline in Lesson 11, "Resource Workloads."

The Set Plan command copies data from scheduled fields into planned fields, for all or selected tasks. With the Set Plan command, you can save up to five additional sets of start and finish dates as interim plans.

Viewing the Schedule

The vertical dashed gridline on the Gantt Chart marks today's date on the timescale. Use the date line to see how far along tasks should be to meet the schedule. Tasks with Gantt bars completely to the left of the date line should be complete. For example, in the following illustration, task 11, "Paint conference room" should be 100% complete.

Tasks whose Gantt bars intersect the date line should be partially complete; for example, task 20, "Install warehouse racks" has already started and should be about 50% complete. Tasks to the right of the date line are scheduled to begin later. None of these tasks appear in this illustration.

Progress bars within the Gantt bars indicate whether a scheduled task is complete, in progress, or has yet to begin. For example, in this illustration, the progress bar for task 11, "Paint conference room," indicates that the task is 100% complete. You can also use the Tracking Form dialog box to view and enter information about a selected task's progress.

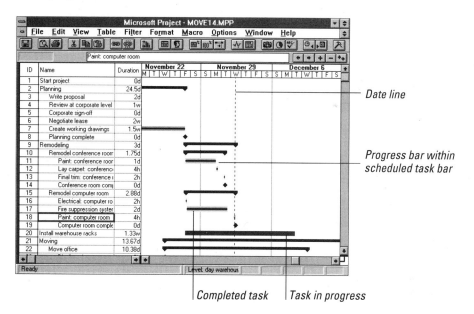

Date line

Progress bar within scheduled task bar

Completed task   Task in progress

Updating the Schedule with Actual Information

Updating your project is an iterative process of modifying the schedule (for tasks that have not yet started) to reflect changes from the original plan, and entering actual information (for tasks that have started), which in turn is incorporated into the schedule for future tasks. You enter actual information as tasks happen. How often you update the schedule depends on how closely you want to track progress.

The Set Actual command on the Options menu makes it easy to enter actual data for tasks that are proceeding according to schedule. For these tasks, the Set Actual command copies data from scheduled fields into actual fields displayed in the Tracking table.

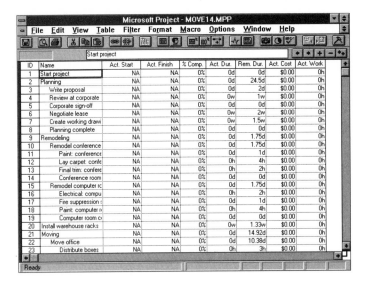

To update tasks that deviate from the schedule, first apply the *Tracking table* to the Task Sheet. This view offers a convenient way to enter actual data, because you can see all of the actual fields at once. You don't need to complete all the actual fields because Microsoft Project can calculate some fields based on the information in other fields. After you enter information in the actual fields, you use the Set Actual command to update the schedule.

You can also change actual data directly on the Gantt Chart by clicking and dragging on the progress bars located within the Gantt bars.

Comparing the Schedule to the Plan

Microsoft Project provides many ways for you to compare your schedule to the plan. You can choose the most convenient method to find out what you need to know.

Apply the Variance table to view the baseline

When you use the Set Plan command, Microsoft Project copies data from scheduled fields into planned fields. Display planned fields by applying the Variance table to the Task Sheet.

1   Hold down SHIFT and choose Task Sheet from the View menu.

2   From the Table menu, choose Variance.

Microsoft Project displays the scheduled and planned date fields in the Task Sheet. The Planned Start and Planned Finish fields contain the dates copied from the Scheduled Start and Scheduled Finish fields when you set the plan.

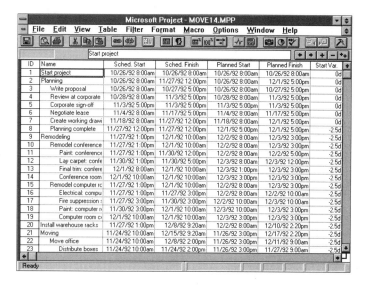

View the schedule with the Gantt Chart

Display the Gantt Chart to get a quick overview.

1   From the <u>V</u>iew menu, choose <u>G</u>antt Chart.

The Gantt Chart indicates today's date with a vertical dashed line, showing you how far along your tasks need to be to stay on schedule.

2   Scroll the task list and timescale to view the rest of the tasks in the project.

Your screen looks like the following illustration.

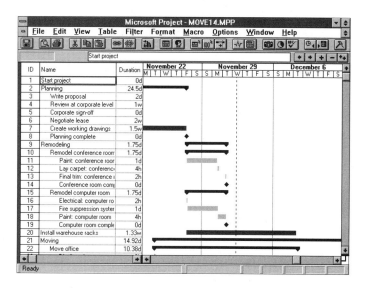

Apply the Tracking table to view actual data

Microsoft Project's Tracking table is a convenient way to view and update data in the actual fields. Use the Tracking table to update the office move schedule with tasks that have finished or are happening now.

1   From the View menu, choose Task Sheet.

The Task Sheet appears.

2   From the Table menu, choose Tracking.

Microsoft Project displays the actual fields in the Task Sheet. "NA" means no actual data has been entered.

Your screen looks like the following illustration.

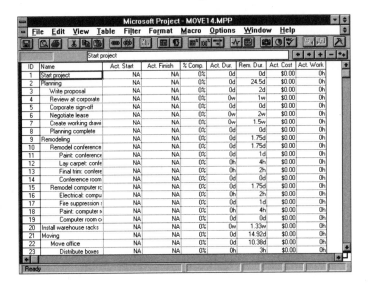

Enter actual data for on-time tasks

The move planning phase and remodeling of the conference room, task 1 through task 14, all started and finished on schedule with the budgeted resources. Save time by using the Set Actual command on the Options menu to automatically enter actual data which is identical to the scheduled data.

1   Select tasks 1 through 14.

2   From the Options menu, choose Set Actual.

The Set Actual dialog box appears. Today's date and time appear in the Update Date box.

3   Select the Selection option to update only selected tasks.

Note that the Set Actual Start and Actual Finish Only option button is selected by default.

4   Choose the OK button.

Microsoft Project copies the data from the Scheduled Start and Scheduled Finish fields into the Actual Start and Actual Finish fields, because the tasks were scheduled to start and finish before today's date.

Update a task that started late

When tasks don't go as scheduled, you need to enter actual data manually. You scheduled the "Electrical: computer room" task to start on 11/27/92 at 1:00 P.M. You found out that the electrician didn't get started until 2:00 P.M. but finished according to the scheduled duration.

Enter actual data for the "Electrical: computer room" task to show that it started and finished one hour late. You can enter 100 in the Percent Complete field, and Microsoft Project calculates the actual finish date and time.

1   Select the Actual Start field for task 16, "Electrical: computer room."

2   Type the correct start time **11/27/92 2:00pm**

3   Click the enter box on the entry bar or press ENTER.

4   In the % Comp. box for "Electrical: computer room," type **100**

Enter 100 percent complete, because the task is finished.

5   Click the enter box on the entry bar or press ENTER.

6   Double-click task 16, to display the Task Edit form.

The Task Edit Form dialog box displays the start and finish times, which do not appear in the Tracking table.

7   Choose the OK button

The Actual Finish field is calculated as 11/27/92 4:00 P.M. The Actual Duration field changes from 0h to 2h, and Remaining Duration field changes from 2h to 0h. Actual Work becomes 2h and Actual Cost is calculated as $40.

Update a task that took longer than scheduled

You originally estimated the "Fire suppression system: computer room" task to take one day. The task started, as scheduled, after the "Electrical: computer room" task, but took two days instead of one. Change the actual duration, and then use the Set Actual command on the Options menu to calculate the actual finish date and time.

1   Select task 17, "Fire suppression system: computer room."

2   In the Actual Duration field box, type **2d**

3   Choose the OK button.

4   From the Options menu, choose Set Actual.

5   Select the Selection option button.

6   Choose the OK button.

The Percent Complete field is 100, the Remaining Duration is 0d, and now the Actual Duration is 2d instead of 1d. Actual Work and Actual Cost are recalculated.

Update a task in progress

The painters were scheduled to start painting the computer room on December 1, but waited until the next day to paint the whole room in one session. They started at 8:00 A.M. and right now are half-finished with the four-hour task.

You need to enter the actual start date manually, because it happened later than scheduled. Then you can enter percent complete to show that the task is half finished.

1   Select the Actual Start field for task 18, "Paint: computer room."

2   Type **12/2/92 8:00am**

3   Click the enter box on the entry bar or press ENTER.

4   In the % Comp. field for task 18, type **50**

5   Click the enter box on the entry bar or press ENTER.

Microsoft Project calculates the actual duration, remaining duration, actual cost, and actual work. Actual finish still displays "NA" because the task is only partially complete.

View actual data in the Gantt Chart

Now that your schedule is updated with actual data on tasks that are finished or under way, you can see progress bars within the schedule bars on the Gantt Chart. The progress bars appear as black lines. When you view the progress bars against the Gantt Chart date line, it's easy to tell whether your project is actually on schedule.

▶   From the View menu, choose Gantt Chart.

Your Gantt Chart looks like the following illustration.

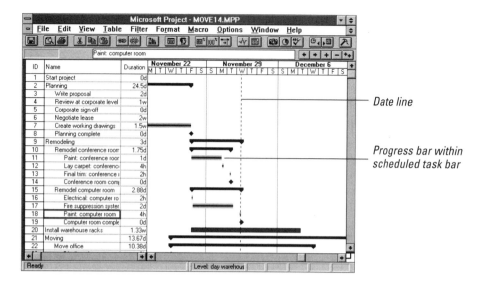

Date line

Progress bar within
scheduled task bar

Comparing Planned vs. Scheduled Data

After the actual data is entered, your schedule is changed significantly. You now need
to compare the current schedule to your plan to see the project's performance. In
addition to the Variance table, which you applied earlier in this lesson, the Tracking
Gantt view allows you to visually compare planned to scheduled progress by displaying Gantt bars for both the planned and current schedule.

Display the Tracking Gantt view

1   From the View menu, choose Define Views.

   The Define Views dialog box appears.

2   In the Views box, select Tracking Gantt.

3   Choose the Set button.

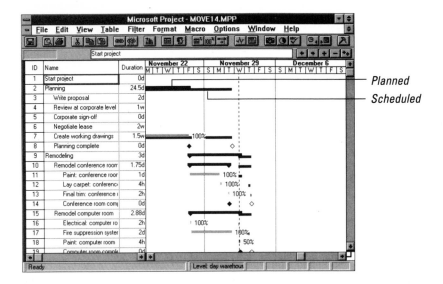

Open the Task Sheet view

▶ From the View menu, choose Task Sheet.

Comparing Planned vs. Actual Data

Use the Work table and Cost table applied to the Task Sheet to compare actual costs and work to what you originally planned.

Display the Work table

The Work table shows planned and actual work.

▶ From the Table menu, choose Work.

Your screen looks like the following illustration.

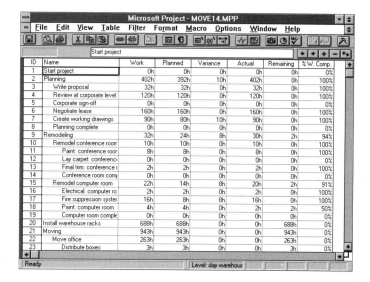

The first screen shows the Work table with columns ID, Name, Work, Planned, Variance, Actual, Remaining, % W. Comp.

ID	Name	Work	Planned	Variance	Actual	Remaining	% W. Comp.
1	Start project	0h	0h	0h	0h	0h	0%
2	Planning	402h	392h	10h	402h	0h	100%
3	Write proposal	32h	32h	0h	32h	0h	100%
4	Review at corporate level	120h	120h	0h	120h	0h	100%
5	Corporate sign-off	0h	0h	0h	0h	0h	0%
6	Negotiate lease	160h	160h	0h	160h	0h	100%
7	Create working drawings	90h	80h	10h	90h	0h	100%
8	Planning complete	0h	0h	0h	0h	0h	0%
9	Remodeling	32h	24h	8h	30h	2h	94%
10	Remodel conference room	10h	10h	0h	10h	0h	100%
11	Paint: conference room	8h	8h	0h	8h	0h	100%
12	Lay carpet: conference	0h	0h	0h	0h	0h	0%
13	Final trim: conference	2h	2h	0h	2h	0h	100%
14	Conference room comp	0h	0h	0h	0h	0h	0%
15	Remodel computer room	22h	14h	8h	20h	2h	91%
16	Electrical: computer ro	2h	2h	0h	2h	0h	100%
17	Fire suppression system	16h	8h	8h	16h	0h	100%
18	Paint: computer room	4h	4h	0h	2h	2h	50%
19	Computer room comple	0h	0h	0h	0h	0h	0%
20	Install warehouse racks	688h	688h	0h	0h	688h	0%
21	Moving	943h	943h	0h	0h	943h	0%
22	Move office	263h	263h	0h	0h	263h	0%
23	Distribute boxes	3h	3h	0h	0h	3h	0%

Display the Cost table

The Cost table shows planned and actual cost.

▶ From the Table menu, choose Cost.

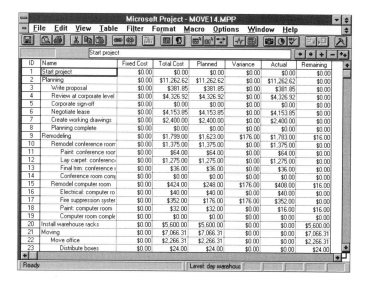

The second screen shows the Cost table with columns ID, Name, Fixed Cost, Total Cost, Planned, Variance, Actual, Remaining.

ID	Name	Fixed Cost	Total Cost	Planned	Variance	Actual	Remaining
1	Start project	$0.00	$0.00	$0.00	$0.00	$0.00	$0.00
2	Planning	$0.00	$11,262.62	$11,262.62	$0.00	$11,262.62	$0.00
3	Write proposal	$0.00	$381.85	$381.85	$0.00	$381.85	$0.00
4	Review at corporate level	$0.00	$4,326.92	$4,326.92	$0.00	$4,326.92	$0.00
5	Corporate sign-off	$0.00	$0.00	$0.00	$0.00	$0.00	$0.00
6	Negotiate lease	$0.00	$4,153.85	$4,153.85	$0.00	$4,153.85	$0.00
7	Create working drawings	$0.00	$2,400.00	$2,400.00	$0.00	$2,400.00	$0.00
8	Planning complete	$0.00	$0.00	$0.00	$0.00	$0.00	$0.00
9	Remodeling	$0.00	$1,799.00	$1,623.00	$176.00	$1,783.00	$16.00
10	Remodel conference room	$0.00	$1,375.00	$1,375.00	$0.00	$1,375.00	$0.00
11	Paint: conference room	$0.00	$64.00	$64.00	$0.00	$64.00	$0.00
12	Lay carpet: conference	$0.00	$1,275.00	$1,275.00	$0.00	$1,275.00	$0.00
13	Final trim: conference	$0.00	$36.00	$36.00	$0.00	$36.00	$0.00
14	Conference room comp	$0.00	$0.00	$0.00	$0.00	$0.00	$0.00
15	Remodel computer room	$0.00	$424.00	$248.00	$176.00	$408.00	$16.00
16	Electrical: computer ro	$0.00	$40.00	$40.00	$0.00	$40.00	$0.00
17	Fire suppression system	$0.00	$352.00	$176.00	$176.00	$352.00	$0.00
18	Paint: computer room	$0.00	$32.00	$32.00	$0.00	$16.00	$16.00
19	Computer room comple	$0.00	$0.00	$0.00	$0.00	$0.00	$0.00
20	Install warehouse racks	$0.00	$5,600.00	$5,600.00	$0.00	$0.00	$5,600.00
21	Moving	$0.00	$7,066.31	$7,066.31	$0.00	$0.00	$7,066.31
22	Move office	$0.00	$2,266.31	$2,266.31	$0.00	$0.00	$2,266.31
23	Distribute boxes	$0.00	$24.00	$24.00	$0.00	$0.00	$24.00

Save button

Save your project and return to the Task Entry view

1   Click the Save button on the tool bar.

2   From the View menu, choose Task Entry.

One Step Further

With the mouse, you can get fast information about a task by clicking the task's Gantt bar. In addition, dragging on the end of the progress bar allows you to change the percent complete. Dragging on the end of the Gantt bar allows you to change the duration. Dragging in the center of the Gantt bar itself lets you change the start date of the task. Try these techniques to change task information.

To make it easier to see the effects of these changes, be sure to click the Timescale Zoom In button on the tool bar until you get the days over hours timescale.

Zoom In button

1   Switch to the Gantt view, then point to the Gantt bar for task 18, "Paint: computer room," and hold down the mouse button.

A dialog box displays information about the task.

Noncritical:	
Scheduled Start:	12/2/92 8:00am
Duration:	4h

2   Point to the right end of the progress bar and hold down the mouse button while you drag to the right until the percent complete is 75%.

When you move to the right end of the progress bar, the cursor looks like the percent arrow below. You might need to click the Timescale Zoom In button on the tool bar once more to make it easier to click on the end of the progress bar.

3   Point to the right end of the Gantt bar and hold down the mouse button while you drag to the right until the duration becomes 12 hours.

When you move to the right end of the Gantt bar, the cursor looks like the right arrow below.

4   Point to the middle of the Gantt bar and hold down the mouse button while you drag to the left until the Scheduled Start is 12/1 6:00 A.M.

When you move to the middle of the Gantt bar, the pointer looks like the double arrow below.

Pointer	Pointer Name
%▸	Percent arrow
▸	Right arrow
◀▢▸	Double arrow

You are not going to save these changes, so feel free to experiment with clicking and dragging on the Gantt bars to see the effect on durations, percent complete, and scheduled start dates.

To get ready for the next lesson, click the Timescale Zoom Out button on the tool bar until you get the weeks over days timescale.

If You Want to Continue to the Next Lesson

Close your project file

1   From the File menu, choose Close.

2   Choose the No button if you see the message box asking whether you want to save your work.

If You Want to Quit Microsoft Project for Now

Quit Microsoft Project

1   From the File menu, choose Exit.

2   Choose the No button if you see the message box asking whether you want to save your work.

Lesson Summary

To	Do this
Save a schedule as a plan	Use the Set Plan command on the Options menu.
Update the schedule with actual data	Use the Set Actual command on the Options menu.
Compare the schedule to the plan	Use the Variance table on the Table menu.
Compare actual data to plan data	Use the Tracking table on the Table menu.

For more information, see in the *Microsoft Project User's Reference*

Options Commands   295

Tables   501

Tracking Progress   567

For an online lesson, see in the Microsoft Project for Windows Online Tutorial

Printing Views and Reports

Tracking Progress

Preview of the Next Lesson

In the next lesson, you'll learn how to reschedule task to meet a deadline. You'll also learn how to recognize critical tasks and use three strategies for shortening the critical path to meet a deadline.

Working with the Critical Path

In this lesson, you'll learn three ways to shorten the critical path, so that you can complete a project faster. You'll change the task relationships of, and add resources to, critical tasks. You'll also learn to adjust the work schedule of resources assigned to critical tasks.

You will learn how to:

- Change task relationships to shorten the critical path.

- Add resources to shorten the critical path.

- Extend workdays to shorten the critical path.

Estimated lesson time: 20 minutes

Start Microsoft Project

If you closed Microsoft Project in the last lesson, you need to restart the application before you can continue.

▶   Double-click the Microsoft Project icon.

Start the lesson

Do the following to open the project file called PRACT15.MPP and rename it MOVE15.MPP.

1   From the File menu, choose Open.

2   In the Directories box, double-click PRACTICE.

3   In the File Name box, double-click PRACT15.MPP.

4   From the File menu, choose Save As.

5   In the File Name box, type **MOVE15.MPP**

6   Choose the OK button.

Microsoft Project stores your project on your hard disk with the filename MOVE15.MPP.

7   Press ALT+HOME to set the timescale at the beginning of the project.

Change today's date and time

Make your project match the screens in this lesson by changing the current date. Use the Project Info command to change your current project date to 12/2/92.

1   From the Options menu, choose Project Info.

     The Project Information dialog box appears.

2   In the Current Date box, select the date and time and type **12/2/92**

3   Choose the OK button.

Crashing the Critical Path

Tasks that cause the project finish date to be delayed if they are not completed as scheduled are said to be on the *critical path*. Tasks on the critical path are called *critical tasks*. When you increase the duration of a critical task, the project is delayed. Similarly, shortening the duration of a critical task causes your project to finish sooner.

Reducing the duration of the critical path is often referred to as *crashing* the critical path. Because critical tasks directly affect the project's finish date, strategies for crashing the critical path focus on reducing task duration. These strategies include:

Changing the relationship between tasks   Shortens the critical path without adding resources or extending work hours.

Scheduling overtime   Shortens the duration.

Adding more resources   Shortens the duration of resource-driven tasks.

Removing unnecessary predecessors   Eliminates delays caused by predecessors that do not affect the task. Make sure all predecessors to critical tasks are essential.

Dealing with the Unexpected

You've just learned the new building has been picked as the site for the annual holiday party. Everything must be in place by noon, December 14.

You have to speed up the move by shortening the critical path. This lesson focuses on reducing the duration of these tasks. First, display the tasks on the critical path, and then try changing the relationships of some tasks.

Filter critical tasks

See which tasks are critical to the project finishing on time.

1   From the Filter menu, choose Critical.

     Critical tasks are displayed.

2   Scroll through the tasks and the timescale until your screen looks like the following illustration.

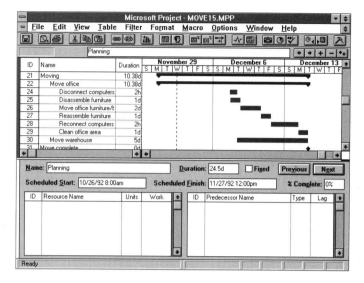

Changing Task Relationships

Defining task relationships more accurately can be the most economical way to shorten the critical path. You may not need to add resources or increase the working hours.

Change the relationship of two tasks

The critical task "Move office furniture/boxes" is not scheduled to begin until "Disassemble furniture" is completely finished. You can start moving boxes and some of the furniture while you are still taking the modular furniture apart. The two tasks can overlap. Change the relationship of these tasks so the move starts when 50 percent of the furniture is disassembled.

1   From the Filter menu, choose All Tasks.

2   Click anywhere in the Task Form to change the active view.

3   From the Format menu, choose Resources & Predecessors.

4   Click in the top view, and select task 26, "Move office furniture/boxes," the successor to "Disassemble furniture."

5   In the Task Form, click the Type field next to "Disassemble furniture."

6   Type **ss** for start-to-start.

7   In the Lag field for "Disassemble furniture," type **50%**

This indicates the second task starts halfway through the schedule of the first.

8   Choose the OK button.

9   Click anywhere in the Gantt chart to make it the active pane.

Zoom In button

10   Click the Timescale Zoom In button once to get a clearer picture of how these tasks overlap.

Look at the Gantt bars to see how the tasks are scheduled now.

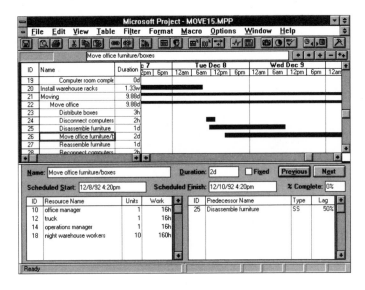

Save button

Save your work

▶ Click the Save button on the tool bar.

View the project finish date

Have these changes moved the project finish date up to the December 14, 12:00 PM. deadline? Use this step to view the finish date.

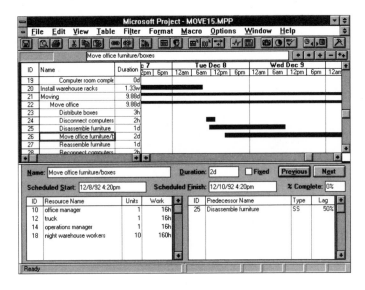

Project Status button

1   Click the Project Status button on the tool bar.

The selected finish date is still December 15. You need to try something else to shorten the schedule.

2   Choose the OK button.

Adding Resources

Despite your best efforts to simplify task relationships, a project might still require that you add resources to a critical task to meet your deadline. However, be prepared to deal with resource overallocation conflicts when you assign more to a task.

Add resources to a task

Because taking down the furniture is a resource-driven task, you can shorten the duration by adding four workers to the task.

1 Select task 25, "Disassemble furniture."

2 Move to the Units column for "day warehouse workers" in the Task Form.

3 To assign a total of six workers, type **6**

4 Choose the OK button.

Microsoft Project adjusts the duration of the task to include the new resources. Notice how the Gantt bars reflect the change.

Level overallocated resources

Because "Disassemble furniture" is resource-driven, Microsoft Project adjusts the task's duration based on the number of resources you assign it. However, notice that the message "Level: day warehouse workers" appears in the status bar. Because other day warehouse workers are already assigned to work on other tasks at the same time that this one is scheduled, they became overallocated when you added the four workers to the "Disassemble furniture" task in the previous step.

Therefore, you need to change the units back to two for the tasks.

1 In the Units field for day warehouse workers, type **2**

2 Choose the OK button.

Changing the Calendar

When adding more resources is not an option for your project, another way to shorten the critical path is to extend the work day or work week. You can change the working hours in the Base Calendar to affect all the resources working on the project.

Increase the working hours

Another task, "Move warehouse," is also on the critical path, and its finish date is December 15. Try shortening this task to bring in the project finish date.

To bring in the finish date of the "Move warehouse" task, make all the resources assigned to the task available for work on the Saturday before the big event.

1 Select task 30, "Move warehouse."

2 From the Options menu, choose Base Calendars.

3 In the Base Calendars box, select Standard.

4 Choose the Edit button.

5 Scroll the calendar to December.

6 Select the last Saturday before December 14.

7 Choose the Working option button.

8 Choose the OK button.

9 Choose the Close button.

Project Status button

View the project finish date

Did increasing the working hours of key resources move the project finish date in to meet the December 14 deadline?

1   Click the Project Status button on the tool bar.

Project Status for MOVE15.MPP		
	Start	Finish
Scheduled	10/26/92 8:00am	12/14/92 9:20am
Planned	10/26/92 8:00am	12/17/92 2:20pm
Actual	NA	NA
Variance	0d	-3.5d

	Duration	Work	Cost
Scheduled	36.17d	2057h	$25,551.93
Planned	38.67d	2047h	$25,551.93
Actual	0d	0h	$0.00
Remaining	36.17d	2057h	$25,551.93

% Complete
Work   0%
Duration   0%

OK

The project finish date is now scheduled for early morning on December 14. It's close, but you can meet your deadline.

2   Choose the OK button to close the Project Status dialog box.

Save button

Save your work

▶   Click the Save button on the tool bar.

One Step Further

Deleting unnecessary predecessors can also save time. To do this effectively, you need to see the predecessors on a Task PERT Chart and analyze the scheduling on the Gantt Chart.

1   Click in the bottom view to change the active view.

2   From the View menu, choose Task PERT.

The Task PERT Chart is displayed in the bottom view.

3   In the Gantt table, select task 28 "Reconnect computers."

The Task PERT Chart displays the predecessor and successor to task 28. This task doesn't need to wait for task 27, "Reassemble furniture." It can begin after the furniture and boxes arrive (task 26).

4   Click anywhere in the bottom view and choose the Task Form from the View menu.

5   In the bottom view, change the predecessor of "Reconnect computers" to be task 26 instead of task 27. You need only enter the task ID number; you do not need to enter the entire task name.

Now make "Reassemble furniture," task 27, the predecessor to "Clean office area" to link "Reassemble furniture" into the schedule.

1   In the Gantt table, select task 29, "Clean office area."

2   Enter task 27, "Reassemble furniture" as its only predecessor, and then choose the OK button.

"Reconnect computers" now begins after "Move office furniture/boxes."

3   Click anywhere in the Gantt Chart to make it active.

4   Click the Timescale Zoom Out button until the timescale displays weeks over days.

If You Want to Continue to the Next Lesson

Save and close your project file

1   From the File menu, choose Close.

2   Choose the Yes button if you see the message box asking whether you want to save your work.

If You Want to Quit Microsoft Project for Now

Save and quit Microsoft Project

1   From the File menu, choose Exit.

2   Choose the Yes button if you see the message box asking whether you want to save your work.

Lesson Summary

To	Do this
Shorten the critical path	Add resources
	Change the relationship of tasks
	Change the base calendar

For more information, see in the *Microsoft Project User's Reference*

Critical Path   69

Scheduling Methods   448

For an online lesson, see in the Microsoft Project for Windows Online Tutorial

Adjusting Schedules

Analyzing the Plan

Preview of the Next Lesson

In the next lesson, you will learn how to prepare and print project information and reports to communicate about the project with other team members and management.

Review & Practice

In the lessons in Part 4, "Controlling the Project," you learned skills to help you become familiar with planning a project. If you want to practice these skills and test your knowledge before you proceed with the lessons in Part 5, you can work through the Review & Practice section following this lesson.

Part 4   Review & Practice

Before you begin planning a project of your own, practice the skills you learned in Part 4 by working through the project management activities in this Review & Practice section. Here you'll respond to changes in the project before the project begins and during the course of the project. You'll also produce a report identifying the cost of a decision affecting a scheduled task.

Scenario

Despite your best efforts to plan every detail of the annual report project, there have been inevitable changes. Some tasks have taken less time than expected, and the president of Victory Sports wants to put his personal touch on the project. So, you will need to add contraints to certain tasks to accommodate his schedule. Use the skills you learned in Part 4 to document these changes, to update the plan, and to ensure that the schedule for the rest of the project takes these changes into account.

You will review and practice how to:

- Update the schedule.
- Record actual data.
- Compare the schedule to the plan.

Estimated practice time: 30 minutes

Before You Begin

1   Open the scenario project called 4ANNUAL.MPP.

2   Save the project file as ANNUAL4.MPP.

3   Press ALT+HOME to set the timescale at the beginning of the project.

This project file should look similar to the file you saved after completing the steps in the Part 3 Review & Practice.

If you see a message telling you that Microsoft Project can't find the Summer base calendar, you need to be sure to do Step 3 in the Part 3 Review and Practice.

Step 1: Shorten the Critical Path

The finish date for the project is currently scheduled for the day of the shareholders meeting. You can see the scheduled finish date with the Project Status command on the Options menu. Because the project goal specifies that the annual reports must be mailed one week before the shareholders meeting, you must shorten the critical path to bring in the finish date on or before September 15.

One way to shorten the critical path is to eliminate unnecessary predecessors for tasks on the critical path. Make the following adjustments to meet the deadline.

- Unlink tasks 6, "Finance," through 9, "President." These tasks do not need to follow one another because several writers can do the interviews at the same time.

- Delete the predecessor in task 15, "Write Articles." The writers do not have to wait for the financial reports to be approved before beginning the articles.

- Delete the predecessor in task 20, "Assemble final materials." Assembly does not have to wait until all the articles have been approved and edited.

- Similarly, specify the predecessor for task 21, "Arrange photographs" to be task 16 "Write first draft." Now the art department can begin selecting photographs as soon as the first drafts have been written.

Verify that you shortened the critical path by choosing the Project Status command from the Options menu. Note the new scheduled finish date.

For more information on	See
Shortening the critical path	Lesson 15

Step 2: Set the Plan

Now that all the tasks have been scheduled so that you are reasonably confident that you can meet the September 15 deadline, use the Set Plan command in the Options menu. Setting a plan now establishes a baseline for future comparisons.

For more information on	See
Setting the plan	Lesson 11

Time Passes...

To simulate the status of your project in progress, change the current date in the Project Information dialog box to August 14, 1992.

Step 3: Enter Actual Data

These tasks took less time then you expected. Use the Set Actual command Selection option after making each of these updates.

Task 2, "Plan articles," required 4 days, not 5.

Task 3, "Assign articles to writers," took 1.5 days, not 2.

Use the Set Actual command All Tasks option to indicate that all other tasks are proceeding according to the schedule. The Scheduled Start and Finish dates will become the Actual Start and Finish dates.

If you have difficulties getting any of these results. be sure that the current date in the Project Info dialog box is set ot 8/14/92.

For more information on	See
Updating the plan with actual data	Lesson 14

Step 4: Update the Schedule

The president wants to add a personal touch this year. He has proposed to sign each cover letter accompanying the annual reports. But he will not be available after September 9, 5:00 P.M.

Insert a new task

Insert a new task before the "Report packets sent" task. Call it "President signs letters." Assign the president as a resource with a rate of $70/h. Because there are over 1000 letters to sign, allow 2 days to complete this task.

Specify a constraint

In the Task Details Edit dialog box specify the constraint Finish No Later Than, and enter the date 9/9/92, 5:00 P.M.

Resolve the scheduling conflict

Link this new task to task 33. Specify a start-to-start relationship and a half-day lag time.

For more information on	See
Inserting a task	Lesson 4
Specifying a task contraint	Lesson 4
Resolving scheduling conflicts	Lesson 13

Step 5: Compare Costs

Starting in the Task Sheet view, apply the Cost table to see cost information and compare scheduled and planned costs.

Apply the Overbudget filter to see only those tasks that are Overbudget.

Double-click on the task "Distribute reports" to display the detail task causing the cost overrun.

For more information on	See
Comparing costs	Lesson 12

Return to the Task Entry view and save your project

Save button

1   From the <u>V</u>iew menu, choose Task <u>E</u>ntry to prepare for the next lesson.

2   Click the Save button on the tool bar.

If You Want to Continue to the Next Lesson

Close your project file

▶   From the <u>F</u>ile menu, choose <u>C</u>lose.

If You Want to Quit Microsoft Project for Now

Quit Microsoft Project

▶   From the <u>F</u>ile menu, choose E<u>x</u>it.

5 Printing and Customizing

Printing Views and Reports

In this lesson, you'll learn several ways to print project information. After you learn how to select the printer on which to print, you will use the page setup command to specify header and footer information, as well as other adjustments to the appearance of the printed page. You will also learn how to preview and print a view and a report.

You will learn how to:

- Select your printer.
- Change the page setup.
- Preview and print a view.
- Preview and print a report.

Estimated lesson time: 40 minutes

Start Microsoft Project

If you closed Microsoft Project in the last lesson, you need to restart the application before you can continue.

▶ Double-click the Microsoft Project icon.

Start the lesson

Do the following to open the project file called PRACT16.MPP and rename it MOVE16.MPP.

1 From the File menu, choose Open.

2 In the Directories box, double-click PRACTICE.

3 In the File Name box, double-click PRACT16.MPP.

4 From the File menu, choose Save As.

5 In the File Name box, type **MOVE16.MPP**

6 Choose the OK button.

   Microsoft Project stores your project on your hard disk with the filename MOVE16.MPP.

7 Press ALT+HOME to set the timescale at the beginning of the project.

Change today's date and time

Make your project match the screens in this lesson by changing the current date. Use the Project Info command to change your current project date to 12/2/92, 10:00 A.M.

1 From the Options menu, choose Project Info.

The Project Information dialog box appears.

2 In the Current Date box, select the date and time and type **12/2/92, 10:00am**

3 Choose the OK button.

Communicating Project Progress

Communicating project plans and progress with the project team and management is critical to executing a successful project plan. Microsoft Project provides many alternatives for conveying project information to those who need to know about your project. Printing views is a fast way to get hard copy of what you see in the active view on your screen. Numerous reports can be printed to give you specialized information. In addition, you can customize views and reports to get the information you need in the format you want.

Setting Up Your Printer with Print Setup

You can print views and reports on the printers you installed on your computer with the Printers program in Windows Control Panel. See your *Microsoft Windows User's Guide* if you need more information about installing printers.

From within Microsoft Project use the Print Setup command on the File menu to select the printer you want to use from the list of installed printers or plotters. You also use this command to change the configuration of the selected printer or plotter. Make sure the printer is set up correctly when you print for the first time. The printer settings are retained, so you don't have to set them again unless you want to change them.

Select a printer

First, make sure the printer or plotter you are using is selected.

1 From the File menu, choose Print Setup.

2 Select the printer you plan to use.

3 Choose the OK button.

Using Page Setup

Use the Page Setup dialog box to set margins, headers, footers, text formats, page orientation, and borders for all types of views and reports. For PERT Charts and Gantt Charts, you can add a legend on the bottom of each page or on a separate legend page.

The following illustration shows the elements you can customize with the Page Setup command.

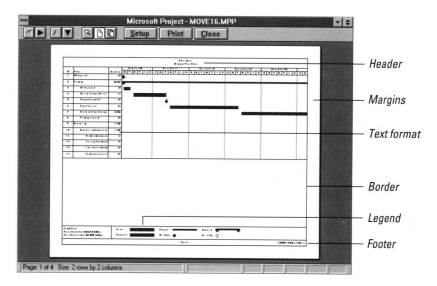

You can enter codes that align the text or embed information into the header, footer, or legend when you print the project. These codes consist of an ampersand (&) followed by a letter that represents the item. For example, &C centers the characters that follow, and &D prints the system date. The following table contains a list you can use in headers, footers, and legends.

Enter this code	To do this
&F	Print name of the project file
&C	Center characters that follow
&L	Align at the left margin characters that follow
&R	Align at the right margin characters that follow
&D	Print current system date
&T	Print current system time
&P	Print page number
&&	Print a single ampersand (&)
&c	Print company name from Project Info dialog box
&d	Print current date from Project Info dialog box
&f	Print project finish date
&s	Print project start date
&m	Print manager's name from Project Info dialog box

Enter this code	To do this
&p	Print project name from Project Info dialog box
&r	Print name of report (for printed reports only)
&v	Print name of view (for printed views only)

Display the page setup for the Gantt Chart

A vice president has requested a report on the current status of the move. You want to show graphically what has been accomplished so far and what is left to do, so print a Gantt Chart view of the project.

You also want to provide the vice president with a summary of the project that can be taken in at a glance. The project summary report provides a one-page summary of the entire project.

Before you print, change the page setup for the Gantt Chart so it is presentation quality and contains all the information management might want.

▶ From the File menu, choose Page Setup.

Gantt Chart is selected in the Page For box. All settings in the Page Setup dialog box apply only to the item selected in the Page For box.

Change the Gantt Chart header and footer

1 Click anywhere in the Header box.

2 Type **&C&p** and press SHIFT+ENTER to move to the next line.

Be sure to use capitalization as noted. You must type a capital "C" and a lowercase "p."

These codes print the project name (&p) from the Project Information dialog box and center it on the page (&C).

3 Type **&CManager: &m**

This entry centers the word "Manager:" followed by the name of the project manager (&m). This is the name of the manager shown in the Project Information dialog box.

4 Select the text in the Footer box, and then type **&CPage: &P&R&d&T**

This entry includes the word "Page:" followed by the page number (&P) at the center (&C) of the page. At the right margin (&R) of the page, it prints the current date (&d) as specified in the Project Information dialog box and the current time (&T) according to your computer's clock.

The Page Setup dialog box looks like the following illustration.

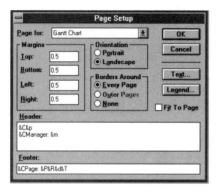

Change the Gantt Chart legend text

Next, add text to the legend to provide explanatory information about the project. By default, the legend prints on every page, but you can also choose to have it print only on the first page, or not to print a legend at all.

1 At the right of the Page Setup dialog box, choose the Legend button.

2 Select the text in the Legend text box.

3 Type **&L&v** and then press SHIFT+ENTER.

These codes print the name of the view (&v) left-aligned (&L) in a box next to the legend.

4 Type **Project start date: &s** and then press SHIFT+ENTER.

This entry includes the text "Project start date:" followed by the project start date (&s) in the box next to the legend. Because no alignment is specified, the text is left-aligned by default.

5 Type **Project finish date: &f**

This entry includes the text "Project finish date:" followed by the project finish date (&f) in the box next to the legend.

The Legend dialog box looks like the following illustration.

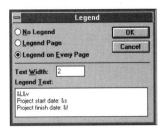

6   Choose the OK button to close the Legend dialog box.

7   Choose the OK button to close the Page Setup dialog box.

Save button

Save your project

▶   Click the Save button on the tool bar.

Previewing and Printing Views

Although you can use the Print command on File menu to print your view right away, it is a good idea to use the Print Preview command first. If you decide you want to make additional adjustments, you can return to the Page Setup dialog box. Otherwise, if you are satisfied with the appearance of the view, you can print the view.

Preview the Gantt Chart view

Use the following steps to examine how the printed pages of the Gantt Chart look before you print the Gantt Chart. You can complete these steps even if you are not connected to a printer.

Print Preview button

1   Click the Print Preview button on the tool bar.

2   To get a close-up view of the task list, click the page.

Now you can read all the tasks.

3   Click the page again, and then click the gray area outside the page.

Now you can see all the pages in the Gantt Chart at the same time as in the following illustration. Your screen may vary slightly from the illustration depending on the type of printer you have installed.

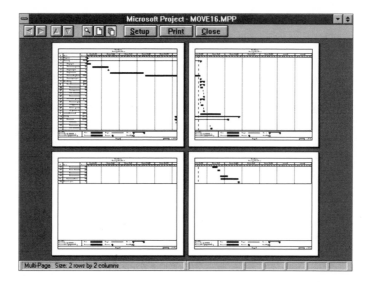

If you decide you want to make additional changes to your margins, header, footer, page orientation, or borders, choose the Setup button to return to the Page Setup dialog box.

Printing Views

A printed view shows only what you see on your screen. You print a view with the Print command on the File menu. You can also use the Print button on the tool bar.

You can print all views except forms and the Task PERT Chart. If you have a combination view displayed on your screen, only the active section of the view is printed.

Print the Gantt Chart view

1   Choose the Print button.

Microsoft Project displays the Print dialog box.

2 If you are connected to a printer, choose the Print button. If you are not connected to a printer, choose the Cancel button.

3 If you chose the Cancel button, choose the Close button to return to your project.

If you choose the Print button, your project prints on the selected printer or plotter. If the printer or plotter prints only one color, Microsoft Project substitutes patterns for colors.

Tip You can adjust the patterns with the Palette command on the Format menu.

Add a page break

If you don't like where the automatic page breaks fall, you can set your own page breaks with the Set Page Break command on the Format menu.

1 Select task 15, "Remodel computer room."

2 From the Format menu, choose Set Page Break.

Microsoft Project inserts a page break, represented by a dashed line, above the selected task.

3 Click the Print Preview button to see what your report looks like now.

4 Click the gray area outside of the page.

Compare your preview screen to the following illustration.

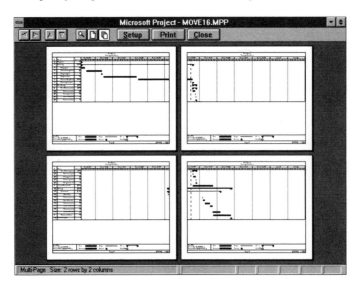

Tip To remove a manual break page, first click in the line below the page break. Then, from the Format menu, choose Remove Page Break.

Previewing and Printing Reports

Using a report, you can print all the information in the project without having to set up your view to display individual sections of the project. Microsoft Project provides five basic reports.

Base Calendar report   Prints information about the base calendars in the current calendar file. For each calendar in the file, the report lists days of the week, working hours, exceptions, and nonworking periods.

Monthly Calendar report   Shows tasks represented as bars (or optionally as lines, or start and end markers) on a monthly calendar.

Project Summary report   Presents a one-page summary of the project. It includes the same information found in the Project Information and Project Status dialog boxes.

Resource report   Provides detailed information about the resources in the project, including scheduled dates, work, and costs for tasks. You also have the option of including base and resource calendar information.

Task report   Provides detailed task information including scheduled dates, work, and costs for resource assignments, as well as task notes, predecessors, and successors.

You can specify a sort order for the report, so you can view your project in one order while you print it in another. Reports include only text and objects such as Microsoft Graph charts. You print a report with the Print Report command on the File menu.

With the Print Report command on File menu you can preview and print your reports. It is a good idea to preview your report before you print it. If you decide you want to make additional adjustments, you can return to the Page Setup dialog box. Otherwise, if you are satisfied with the appearance of the report, you can print it.

Print the summary report

In addition to the Gantt Chart, you want to give the vice president the project summary report. This report provides a one-page summary of the major project details, such as number of tasks and resources, start and end dates, and other project-wide information found in the Project Information and Project Status dialog boxes. You cannot change the content of the project summary report. Now print the summary report to accompany the Gantt Chart.

1   From the File menu, choose Print Report.

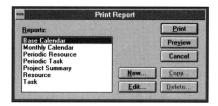

2   In the Reports box, select Project Summary.

3   Click the Preview button to see what your report looks like.

4   Click on the page to get a close view of the report.

Your summary report looks like the following illustration.

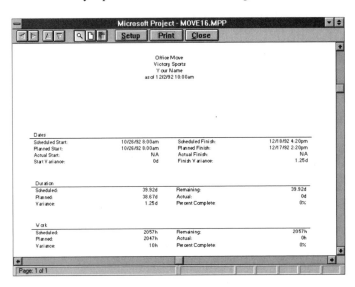

5   If you are connected to a printer, choose the Print button. Choose the Close button if you are not going to print the report.

Print the monthly calendar report

Although management appreciates the concise nature of the project summary report, your project team members need more information about what is expected of them and about other tasks that are going on at the same time. For them, the monthly calendar report is especially useful, because it consists of a monthly calendar with Gantt bars showing when tasks are scheduled to occur in the month.

1   From the File menu, choose Print Report.

2   In the Reports box, select Monthly Calendar.

3   Choose the Print button to display the Print dialog box.

4   Under Timescale, select the Manual option button.

5   In the From box, type **11/1/92**

6   In the To box, type **11/30/92**

7   Choose the Preview button.

8 Click the page to focus on the tasks in November.

Each task is represented by a bar on the calendar. You can show tasks as bars, lines, or start and finish dates by selecting a different format in the Monthly Calendar Report Definition dialog box.

9 If you are connected to a printer, choose the Print button. If you are not connected to a printer, choose the Close button.

Your printed monthly calendar report looks like the following illustration.

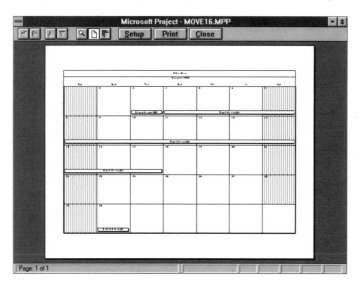

Save button

Save your project

▶ Click the Save button on the tool bar.

One Step Further

You can also change the font name, size, and style of the header, footer, and legend text to make information stand out better.

1 From the File menu, choose Page Setup.

2 In the Page For box, select Gantt Chart if not already selected.

3 Choose the Text button.

4 In the Item To Change box, select Header (top).

5 Select the Bold check box.

6 In the Item To Change box, select Header (middle).

7 Select the Bold check box.

The two lines of the Gantt Chart header now print in bold.

8 Choose the OK button.

9 Choose the OK button again.

10 Click the Print Preview button on the tool bar to preview the view.

Print Preview button

11 If you are satisfied with your view and are connected to a printer, click the Print button to print the view or choose the Close button.

If You Want to Continue to the Next Lesson

Save and close your project file

1 From the File menu, choose Close.

2 Choose the Yes button if you see the message box asking whether you want to save your work.

If You Want to Quit Microsoft Project for Now

Save and quit Microsoft Project

1 From the File menu, choose Exit.

2 Choose the Yes button if you see the message box asking whether you want to save your work.

Lesson Summary

To	Do this
Change the headers, footers, and legends for views and reports	Choose the Page Setup command from the File menu. Use codes to embed and format project information to print on the first or every page of the printed view.
Preview a view or report	Click the Print Preview button on the tool bar to see a reduced representation of the active view that you are going to print. Buttons on the preview screen allow you to Print or to go to the Page Setup dialog box.
Select a printer	Choose the Print Setup command fromthe File menu. Select a printer from the list of printers installed on your computer.
Print a view	Click the Print button on the tool bar.
Print a report	Choose the Print Report command from the File menu. Select from list of reports the one you want to print.

For more information, see in the *Microsoft Project User's Reference*

Printing and Plotting   336

Reports   364

For an online lesson, see in the Microsoft Project for Windows Online Tutorial

Printing Reports

Preview of the Next Lesson

In the next lesson, you will learn how to create and print your own customized reports. You will combine many of the same techniques you have already learned for filtering and formatting views with new features to get the information you need.

Customizing Tables and Reports

In this lesson, you'll learn how to create tables and reports to meet your specialized information requirements. First, you'll change the appearance of text and charts. You'll also create a custom table based on a copy of an existing table. Finally, you'll create an original custom report.

You will learn how to:

- Format text and charts.
- Create a custom table.
- Create a custom report.

Estimated lesson time: 30 minutes

Start Microsoft Project

If you closed Microsoft Project in the last lesson, you need to restart the application before you can continue.

▶   Double-click the Microsoft Project icon.

Start the lesson

Do the following to open the project file called PRACT17.MPP and rename it MOVE17.MPP.

1   From the File menu, choose Open.

2   In the Directories box, double-click PRACTICE.

3   In the File Name box, double-click PRACT17.MPP.

4   From the File menu, choose Save As.

5   In the File Name box, type **MOVE17.MPP**

6   Choose the OK button.

   Microsoft Project stores your project on your hard disk with the filename MOVE17.MPP.

7   Press ALT+HOME to set the timescale at the beginning of the project.

Change today's date and time

Make your project match the screens in this lesson by changing the current date. Use the Project Info command to change your current project date to 12/2/92, 10:00 A.M.

1   From the Options menu, choose Project Info.

The Project Information dialog box appears.

2   In the Current Date box, select the date and time and type **12/2/92 10:00am**

3   Choose the OK button.

Formatting a Table

Adding custom formatting to the view makes it easier to read and more attractive. In Microsoft Project you can format the appearance of text in all tables and reports. For example, to draw attention to specific tasks, you can format them bold. To make progress bars appear more clearly, you can change the pattern of the Gantt bars. To better illustrate the structure of your plan, you can show outline numbers in the Gantt table.

Format the table text

In Lesson 6, you created filters to display information for your monthly report to the managers. Now you need to print the report for the managers' meeting. First, format the text in the table to make it easier to distinguish between summary tasks, milestones, and subordinate tasks.

1   From the Format menu, choose Text.

2   In the Item To Change box, select Summary Tasks.

3   Select the Bold check box.

4   Select the Underline check box.

5   In the Item To Change box, select Milestone Tasks.

6   Select the Bold check box.

7   Select the Italic check box.

8   Choose the OK button.

Enlarge the Gantt Chart

▶   Hold down SHIFT and choose Gantt Chart from the View menu for a single-pane view to better show the results of your changes.

Your screen looks like the following illustration.

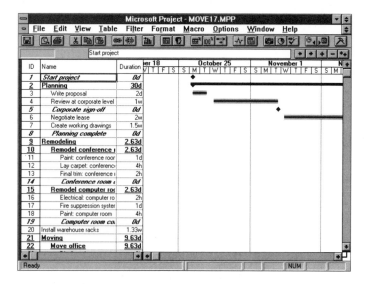

Format symbols on the Gantt Chart

1 From the Format menu, choose Palette.

You can also double-click the Gantt Chart outside a Gantt bar. The Palette dialog box appears.

2 Select Critical.

Changes you make to the Gantt bars will now apply to all critical tasks.

3 In the Pattern box under Bar, select the pattern identified in the illustration which follows this step.

The sample critical bar at the top of the Palette table shows the pattern you selected.

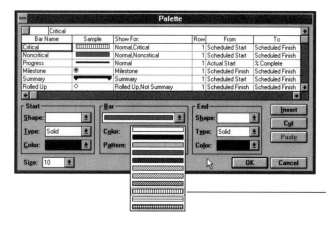

Pattern to select is highlighted

4   Scroll the Palette table to the right to display the Left Text column.

5   In the Left Text column, select the second field.

This is the Left Text field for noncritical tasks. Left text appears on the left of a Gantt bar to provide additional information about a task.

6   In the entry bar list, located in the upper-left corner of the Palette dialog box, click the arrow and select Free Slack from the drop-down list.

Free slack is the amount of time a task can be delayed without delaying another task.

7   Choose the OK button.

8   Scroll task 12 to the top of the task list. Scroll the timescale to the week of Nov. 22, 1992.

Your Gantt Chart should look like the following illustration.

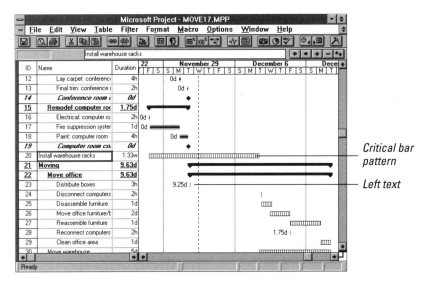

Display outline numbers

1   From the Format menu, choose Outline.

2   Select the Outline Number check box.

3   Choose the OK button.

Your Gantt table now contains outline numbers as shown in the following illustration.

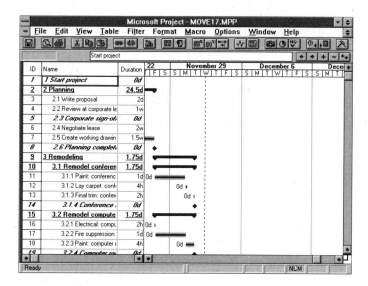

Creating a Custom Table

Although the existing tables and reports supplied with Microsoft Project usually meet most of your reporting needs, you might have specialized information requirements. With Microsoft Project, you can modify existing reports and tables, or you can create entirely new ones.

At Victory Sports, you use the same information every month to produce your reports. To save time in the future, create a custom table that contains only the columns you need. Because the table you want to create is similar to the existing Summary table, you can make your changes to a copy of the Summary table.

Copy the existing Summary table

1   From the Table menu, choose Define Tables.

The Task box contains a list of Task tables.

2   In the Tables box, select Summary.

3   Choose the Copy button.

Microsoft Project makes a copy of the Summary table and displays the Table Definition dialog box.

4   In the Name box, type **Monthly Report**

This entry names the new table you are creating.

Customize the new table

You're now ready to change the columns in your custom copy of the table. You can delete the ID column because tasks are already identified by the outline numbers you just set up. To accommodate these outline numbers, you also need to widen the Name column.

1   In the Field Name column, click the name ID.

2   Choose the Delete button.

3   In the Width field, select the width for the Name field.

4   Type **32**

5   Click the enter box on the entry bar or press ENTER.

The Table Definition dialog box now looks like the following illustration.

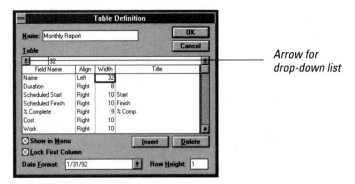

Arrow for drop-down list

Unlock the first column

In the table you copied, the first column was "locked." Locking keeps a column in place on the screen, so it's always visible even when you scroll left or right to see other columns. It also prevents you from making changes in the locked column. Because you do want to edit the Name column, you need to unlock it.

▶ Clear the Lock First Column check box.

Change a column and apply the table

Because you and your team are more interested in seeing resource names than work information, change the Work column on the Summary table to resource names instead.

1 In the Field Name column, select Work.

2 Use the arrow in the entry bar to scroll to Resource Names.

3 Choose the OK button.

4 Choose the Set button.

Apply a filter to show one month

You want to show only the activities that took place during November, so apply the Date Range filter.

1 From the Filter menu, choose Date Range.

2 In the First Date box, type **11/1/92**

3 In the Last Date box, type **11/30/92**

4 Choose the OK button.

5 Scroll to the first two weeks in November.

  You can also press F5 to display the Go To dialog box and enter a date you want.

Print the view

You can now print the view. You print it the same way you printed views in Lesson 16.

1 From the File menu, choose Print.

  The Print dialog box appears.

2 If you are connected to a printer, choose the Print button.

  If you are not connected to a printer, choose the Preview button to see how the printed pages look.

Compare your preview screen to the following illustration.

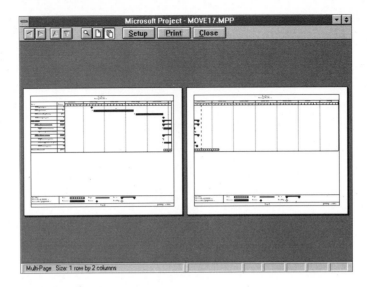

3   After previewing, choose the Close button.

Creating a Custom Report

In this month's managers' meeting, you want to supplement your monthly report with a report on cost overruns—tasks that are over budget. Create a new report that uses the Overbudget filter and the Cost table. Name the custom report and print it using the Print Report command on the File menu.

Create and name a new report

1   From the File menu, choose Print Report.

2   Choose the New button.

3   Choose the OK button to select Task in the Report Type box.

The new report is going to be a task report.

4   In the Name box, type **Overruns**

5   In the Table box, select Cost.

6   In the Filter box, select Overbudget.

7   Under Assignments, select the Cost check box.

This selection prints cost fields for the resource assignments of each task.

8   Select the Print Totals check box.

This selection includes project totals on the report.

9   Select the Print Gray Bands check box.

This selection displays a patterned band between each task so it's easier to see where the information for each task ends.

10   Choose the OK button.

Print the custom report

You can print the report directly from the Print Report dialog box.

1   Choose the Print button, if you are connected to a printer.

2   If you are not connected to a printer, choose the Preview button to see how the printed pages look.

Your report looks like the following illustration.

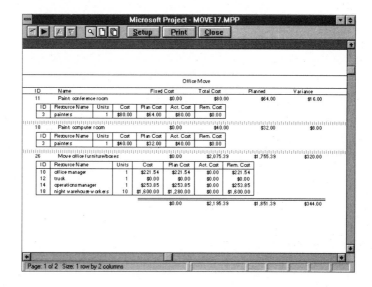

3   After previewing, choose the Close button.

One Step Further

One of the most powerful ways to tailor your custom reports is to include interactive filters in them. Whenever you print, interactive filters prompt you to specify the particular project information you want to see in the report.

   1   From the File menu, choose Print Report.

   2   Choose the New button.

   3   Choose the OK button to create a task report.

   4   In the Name box, type **Weekly Schedule**

   5   In the Table box, select Schedule.

   6   In the Filter box, select Date Range.

   7   Choose the OK button.

   8   Choose the Print button.

   9   Choose the Print button again.

         A dialob box appears, prompting you for the date range to print.

   10 Type a date range, and then choose the OK button, or choose the Cancel button to cancel printing.

If You Want to Continue to the Next Lesson

Save and close your project file

   1   From the File menu, choose Close.

   2   Choose the Yes button if you see the message box asking whether you want to save your work.

If You Want to Quit Microsoft Project for Now

Save and quit Microsoft Project

   1   From the File menu, choose Exit.

   2   Choose the Yes button if you see the message box asking whether you want to save your work.

Lesson Summary

To	Do this
Format text	Choose the Text command from the Format menu. Select what you want to change from the Item To Change box. Then choose the font, font size, and style.
Format charts	Choose the Palette command from the Format menu. Select the chart element you want to change, and make selections in the Shape, Type, Pattern, and Color boxes.

To	Do this
Create a custom table	Choose the Define Tables command from the Table menu. Choose the Copy button to make a new table based on an existing table. Choose the Edit button to modify an existing table. Choose the New button to create a new table not based on an existing table.
Create a custom report	Choosethe Print Report command from the File menu. Choose the Copy button to make a new report based on an existing report. Choose the Edit button to modify an existing report. Choose the New button to create a new report not based on an existing report.

For more information, see in the *Microsoft Project User's Reference*

Columns   32

Formatting Text   62

Gantt Chart   165

Gridlines   191

Reports   364

Sorting Information   474

Tables   501

Views   632

For an online lesson, see in the Microsoft Project for Windows Online Tutorial

Changing the Look

Printing Views and Reports

Preview of the Next Lesson

In the next lesson, you'll learn how to save changes in another view file (other than the default VIEW.MPV). You'll open and modify alternative view files, and create and save new view files of your own.

Customizing Views and View Files

In this lesson, you'll learn how Microsoft Project makes it easy to customize and create your own views. First, you'll open and explore views in a sample view file called COST.MPV. Then, you'll change the specific settings for a view, as well as for tables, filters, and reports. Finally, you'll save these changes in a view file of your own.

You will learn how to:

- Open a sample view file.
- Create a custom view.
- Save view changes.

Estimated lesson time: 20 minutes

Start Microsoft Project

If you closed Microsoft Project in the last lesson, you need to restart the application before you can continue.

▶   Double-click the Microsoft Project icon.

Start the lesson

Do the following to open the project file called PRACT18.MPP and rename it MOVE18.MPP.

1   From the File menu, choose Open.

2   In the Directories box, double-click PRACTICE.

3   In the File Name box, double-click PRACT18.MPP.

4   From the File menu, choose Save As.

5   In the File Name box, type **MOVE18.MPP**

6   Choose the OK button.

Microsoft Project stores your project on your hard disk with the filename MOVE18.MPP.

7   Press ALT+HOME to set the timescale at the beginning of the project.

Change today's date and time

Make your project match the screens in this lesson by changing the current date. Use the Project Info command to change your current project date to 12/2/92, 10:00 A.M.

1   From the Options menu, choose Project Info.

The Project Information dialog box appears.

2   In the Current Date box, select the date and time and type **12/2/92, 10:00am**

3   Choose the OK button.

Using Alternate View Files

Microsoft Project presents project information using views. Views determine what project information you see, and the format and styles in which information is presented. The specific settings for your views—as well as for tables, filters, reports, custom edit form dialog boxes, macros, and the tool bar—are stored in *view files*. Any changes you make to the appearance of your project are stored in the default view file. Whenever you open any project file, new or existing, it will be displayed in the default view, with the most recent changes to the view in effect.

In addition to the default view file, VIEW.MPV, Microsoft Project supplies nine more sample view files. Each view file contains a set of views that you might find useful for addressing different project management issues while working in Microsoft Project.

Some sample view files are stored in the Microsoft Project applications directory (called WINPROJ). In addition, all the view files are stored in the LIBRARY subdirectory of WINPROJ. Appendix C contains a brief description of each of the sample view files.

Even with all these views, you might prefer using your own views and view combinations. Microsoft Project makes it easy to customize and create your own views.

Open a custom view file

1   From the View menu, choose Define Views.

2   Choose the Open button.

3   In the Directories box, double-click WINPROJ.

4   In the Directories box, double-click LIBRARY.

5   In File Name box, double-click COST.MPV.

The views in the COST.MPV file help you enter and view information associated with costs.

6   Choose the OK button to replace the current file with the new view file.

7   In the View box, select Cost Gantt.

8   Choose the Set button.

Your view looks like the following illustration.

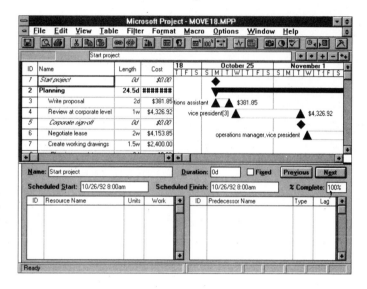

Open the default view file

To use the default view again, open VIEW.MPV.

1   From the View menu, choose Define Views.

2   Click the Open button.

3   In the Directories box, double-click WINPROJ.

4   In the File Name box, double-click VIEW.MPV.

5   Choose the OK button to replace the current view file with the default view file VIEW.MPV.

6   In the View box, select Gantt Chart.

7   Choose the Set button.

Saving and Opening Views

You save and open view files with the Define Views command on the View menu. Any set of tables, filters, reports, views, macros, custom forms, and tool bar can be saved in a view file. A view file also saves the formats you select using the Format menu. For example, all the changes you have made in these lessons are saved in the default view file called VIEW.MPV.

If you don't save your changes to a different view file, your changes are saved to VIEW.MPV when you quit Microsoft Project. If you save changes in VIEW.MPV, these changes are used as the defaults the next time you start Microsoft Project.

Customizing Views

Customizing a view means setting up a view to meet your specific needs. Anytime you change the appearance of the screen you are customizing the view. Outlining, applying filters and tables, sorting tasks, formatting, and reports can all be part of the views you define.

If there is a collection of adjustments you make regularly, you can save time by defining a new view. The next time you want to display the screen in this particular manner, you need only choose your defined view from the menu. If there are specific views that you use at the same time, you define new combination views. You can customize views to include reports and tables you use together.

With the Define Views command on the View menu, you can set up custom views and save them for future use.

Create a custom view

To avoid applying a table and filter to a view each time you want to customize it, you can create a custom view that automatically applies the table and filter. You base your custom view on the views supplied with Microsoft Project, such as the Gantt Chart, PERT Chart, Resource Form, or Task Sheet.

1   From the View menu, choose Define Views.

The Define Views dialog box appears. Because the Gantt draft is selected, the new view will be based on the Gantt chart.

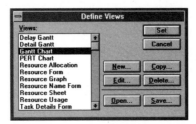

2   Choose the New button.

The Define New View dialog box appears.

3   Choose the OK button to create a single-pane view.

The View Definition dialog box appears.

4   In the Name box, type **Monthly Reports**

Your new chart is based on the Gantt Chart, which is the default in the Screen box. You don't have to select a different screen.

5   In the Table box, select Monthly Report.

6   In the Filter box, select Date Range.

7   Choose the OK button.

8   Choose the Set button.

When you apply the view, the Date Range filter displays the Date Range dialog box, which asks you for the date range to display in the view.

Because the Victory Sports moving project is in its final stages in December, look at December's information.

9   In the First Date box, type **12/1/92**

10   In the Last Date box, type **12/31/92**

11   Choose the OK button.

12 Scroll the timescale to display the first two weeks of December.

Your screen looks like the following illustration. The task list displays only those tasks that start on or after December 1.

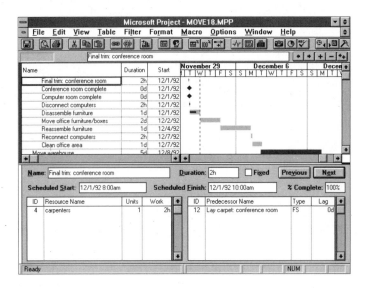

Saving a Custom View

Usually, all the changes you make are saved in the VIEW.MPV file when you quit Microsoft Project. If the changes you make—along with the tables and reports you created—are specific to a particular use and you use them only occasionally, you can save them in a different view file. Whenever you want to use your custom views, tables, reports, and tool bar again, you open the new view file instead of VIEW.MPV.

Save view changes to a different view file

1 From the View menu, choose Define Views.

2 Choose the Save button.

3 In the File Name box type **monthly**

View files are automatically saved with the extension MPV.

4 Choose the OK button.

5 Choose the Close button.

One Step Further

To prepare for meetings with individual resources in which you plan to concentrate on tasks in progress, create a new version of the Periodic Task report that is based the Monthly Reports table you created in Lesson 17, "Customizing Tables and Reports."

Make this report easier to read by formatting highlighted tasks to be bold and italic.

1   From the File menu, choose Print Report.

2   Choose the New button.

3   In the Reports box, select Periodic Task.

4   Choose the OK button to create a new periodic task report.

The Periodic Report Definition dialog box appears.

5   In the Name box, type **Weekly Progress**

6   In the Table box, select Monthly Report.

7   In the Filter box, select In Progress.

8   Check the Highlight box so that the report highlights the tasks in progress.

9   Choose the Text button.

10   In the Text dialog box, select Highlighted Tasks, and check the Bold and Italic check boxes.

With the highlighted tasks in bold and italic, your report is easier to read.

11   Choose the OK button to return to the Period Report Definition dialog box.

12   Choose the OK button to return to the Print Report dialog box.

13   Choose the Print button to print your report, or choose the Preview button to preview your new report.

14   In the Print dialog box or the Print Preview window, choose the Print button, or choose the Close button to cancel printing.

If You Want to Continue to the Next Lesson

Save and close your project file

1   From the File menu, choose Close.

2   Choose the Yes button if you see the message box asking whether you want to save your work.

If You Want to Quit Microsoft Project for Now

Save and quit Microsoft Project

1   From the File menu, choose Exit.

2   Choose the Yes button if you see the message box asking whether you want to save your work.

Lesson Summary

To	Do this
Open sample view files	Choose the Define Views command from the Views menu. Choose the Open button to see a list of view files.
Create a custom view	Choose the Define Views command from the Views menu. Choose the Edit button to make changes to an existing view. Choose the Copy button to make a copy of an existing view and then edit it. Choose the New button to create a new view not based on an existing view.
Save view changes to a new view file	Choose the Define Views command from the Views menu. After creating or modifying views, choose the Save button. In the File Name box, enter the new view file name.

For more information, see in the *Microsoft Project User's Reference*

Filters   131

Formatting Text   162

Reports   164

Tables   501

Views   632

For an online lesson, see in the Microsoft Project for Windows Online Tutorial

Changing the Look

Printing Views and Reports

Preview of the Next Lesson

In the next lesson, you will learn how to tailor Microsoft Project to your personal work style. You will assign a frequently-used command to a button on the tool bar so that you can choose the command with a single click. You will also use a built-in macro to do multiple operations with a single command.

Customizing the Project Environment

In this lesson, you will learn how Microsoft Project allows you to customize the way you use the program itself. As an example of the extent to which you can customize Microsoft Project, you will open the view file EASY.MPV. You will also run a built-in macro to demonstrate how Microsoft Project lets you combine commands. Finally, you will add and modify buttons on the tool bar to give you even easier access to commonly used commands.

You will learn how to:

- Change a view name on the View menu.
- Run a built-in macro.
- Assign a command to a button on the tool bar.

Estimated lesson time: 30 minutes

Start Microsoft Project

If you closed Microsoft Project in the last lesson, you need to restart the application before you can continue.

▶   Double-click the Microsoft Project icon.

Start the lesson

Do the following to open the project file called PRACT19.MPP and rename it MOVE19.MPP.

1   From the File menu, choose Open.

2   In the Directories box, double-click PRACTICE.

3   In the File Name box, double-click PRACT19.MPP.

4   From the File menu, choose Save As.

5   In the File Name box, type **MOVE19.MPP**

6   Choose the OK button.

   Microsoft Project stores your project on your hard disk with the filename MOVE19.MPP.

7   Press ALT+HOME to set the timescale at the beginning of the project.

Changing a Custom View

The EASY.MPV view file contains views in which the view names have been modified to reflect ordinary business terms rather than project management terminology. For example, the Resource Sheet has been renamed "Employee Information." In addition, the views themselves have been changed to use larger–sized text and highlight filters to emphasize summary tasks.

Open the EASY.MPV view file

Do the following to open the EASY.MPV view file. Then open several views to see how they can help you organize your projects.

1   From the View menu, choose Define Views.

2   In the Define Views dialog box, choose the Open button.

3   In the Directories box, double-click LIBRARY.

4   In the File Name box, select EASY.MPV.

5   Choose the OK button.

6   In the Open View File dialog box, select the Replace option.

This selection does not remove the VIEW.MPV view file from your computer. You are only replacing the set of views you have available at this time. To return to your usual views, simply open the VIEW.MPV view file.

7   Choose the OK button to update the View menu.

8   Choose the Close button to return to your project.

Open the Employee Information view

▶   From the View menu, choose Employee Information.

The Employee Information view is displayed. Originally this view was the Resource Sheet, containing basic resource information for a project. In this new view, you see that the size of the text has been enlarged to make it easier to read.

Your view looks like the following illustration.

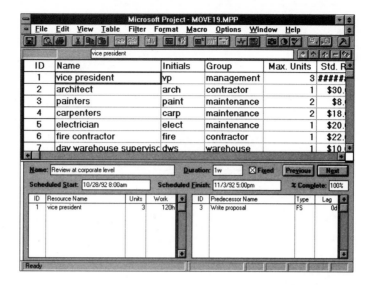

Customize the view name

Victory Sports' human resources vice president prefers to use the word "people" instead of "employees." Follow these steps to change the "Employees Information" view to be called "PeopleInfo" to reflect this preference.

1 From the View menu, choose Define Views.

2 With Employee Information still selected, choose the Edit button.

3 In the Name box, type **&PeopleInfo**

The "&" in front of the "P" means that this letter is now underlined in the View menu.

4 Choose the OK button to return to the Define Views dialog box.

5 Choose the Set button to open this view.

6 Select the View menu.

Notice that the Employee Information view name has been changed to PeopleInfo.

Your View menu looks like the following illustration.

Set another view

Another view that you and your project team might find useful is the Task Sheet. In the EASY.MPV view file, the Task Sheet has been renamed the To Do list. This name reflects a common understanding of how the information on the Task Sheet is used.

▶ From the View menu, choose To Do List.

In this new view, you see that the text has been enlarged to make it easier to read.

Your view looks like the following illustration.

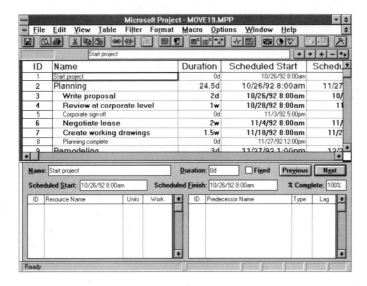

Customizing the Tool Bar

To make it even easier to open the views you need, you can assign the view to a button, and then place the button on the tool bar. Now you can open a view with the click of a button on the tool bar rather than by making several menu selections. In the next steps, you open the view file you saved in the previous lesson and assign a view to a button on the tool bar. You can make it even easier to open the Monthly Reports view by simply clicking the button on the tool bar.

Open a custom view file

1 From the View menu, choose Define Views.

2 Choose the Open button.

3 If you see a message box asking whether you want to save changes to the EASY.MPV file, choose No.

4 In the Directories box, select the WINPROJ directory.

5 Double-click MONTHLY.MPV.

6   Choose the OK button to replace the current file with the new view file.

7   In the View box, select Gantt Chart.

8   Choose the Set button.

Customize the tool bar

Use the following steps to place a new button on the tool bar. Depending on your display settings, your tool bar may not show enough space to hold additional buttons. Step 5 explains how to create additional space on the tool bar if you need it.

Hammer button

1   Hold down CTRL, and then click to the right of the Hammer button on the far right on the tool bar.

The Button Definition dialog box appears.

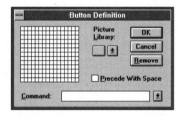

2   In the Command box, select View from the list.

3   Click to the right of the "w" after the word "View" and type a space, then type **"Monthly Reports"**

The quotation marks are required.

4   In the Picture Library box, scroll the list to select a different picture.

5   Choose the OK button.

The new button is shown to the right of the Hammer button.

If your new button does not completely fit on the tool bar, you can make room by removing extra space. Press SHIFT and click a button to remove the space next to it. Depending on your display settings, you may need to remove several spaces to add buttons.

Calculator button

6   Hold down the SHIFT key and drag the new button to the right of the Calculator button.

Review the month of November using the new button

1   Click the new button on the tool bar to change to the Monthly Reports view.

The Date Range filter again displays a dialog box asking for the range to display in the Monthly Reports view.

2 In the First Date box, type **11/1/92**

3 In the Last Date box, type **11/30/92**

4 Choose the OK button.

5 Scroll the timescale to the end of November,1992.

Open the default view file

To use the default view again without any of your custom features, open VIEW.MPV.

1 From the View menu, choose Define Views.

2 Choose the Open button.

3 Save changes to MONTHLY.MPV.

4 Double-click VIEW.MPV.

5 Choose the OK button to replace MONTHLY.MPV with VIEW.MPV.

6 In the Views box, select Task Entry.

7 Choose the Set button.

Understanding Macros

A *macro* is simply a series of commands performed in a sequence that you initiate with a single command. When you find that you often repeat the same set of commands, such as you might do when creating month-end reports, you can create a macro that carries out these commands. Then, at the end of the month, you can run the macro, and have Microsoft Project create the reports for you.

Microsoft Project supplies many macros to help you perform common operations. In this lesson, you learn how to run a built-in macro. If you have unique needs not addressed with any of the built-in macros, you can create your own.

Note   You can get step–by–step instructions for creating your own macros, as well as detailed descriptions of the macro commands and instructions for using them in macros, in two documents—MACRO.WRI and COMMANDS.WRI. You can open these documents using the Write program in the Accessories group in Windows. See your *Microsoft Windows User's Guide* for more information about using Write.

Running a Macro

To run a macro, you select the macro you want from the Macro menu. If you want a description of what the macro does, you can open the macro and read the comments about it in the Macro Definition dialog box.

Learn about a macro

Do the following to read the description about a macro.

1   From the Macro menu, choose Define Macro.

The Define Macros dialog box appears.

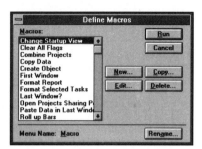

2   In the Macros box, scroll to and select the macro called Search Notes in the list box.

3   Choose the Edit button.

The Macro Definition dialog box appears.

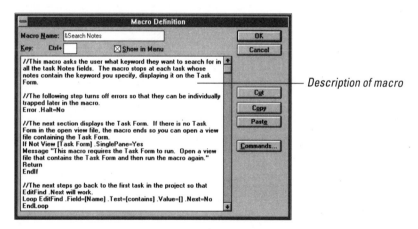

— *Description of macro*

4   After reading the description, choose the Cancel button to return to the Define Macros dialog box, and then choose the Cancel button to close the Define Macros dialog box.

Run a macro

1   From the Macro menu, choose Search Notes.

2   In the EditFind Value dialog box, type **Discuss**

3   Choose the OK button.

The macro searches for and then displays the Task Form for each task that contains the word "Discuss" in the Notes box. After each task is displayed, a message box asks you if you want to see the next task.

4   Choose the Yes button to display the next task.

After all the tasks have been displayed, you see a message box indicating that you have seen all tasks matching your search criteria. The last task found is displayed.

Return to the Task Entry view

▶   From the <u>V</u>iew menu, choose Task <u>E</u>ntry.

One Step Further

To make running a macro even easier, you can assign it to a button and place it on the tool bar. Assign the Search Notes macro to a button and place it on the tool bar.

Hammer button

1   Hold down CTRL, and then click the Hammer button on the far right on the tool bar.

2   In the Command box, select Macro from the list.

3   Click to the right of the "o" after the word "Macro," and then type a space followed by **"Search Notes"**

The quotation marks are required.

4   In the Picture Library box, scroll the list to select a different picture.

5   Choose the OK button.

The picture on the button in the tool bar changes to the picture you selected.

If your new button does not completely fit on the tool bar, you can make room by removing space on the tool bar. Press SHIFT and click a button to remove the space next to it.

6   Click the new button on the tool bar to run the Search Notes macro.

7   In the EditFind Value dialog box, type **class**

8   Choose the OK button.

The macro searches for and then displays the Task Form for each task that contains the word "Class" in the Notes box. After each task is displayed, a message box asks you if you want to see the next task.

9   Choose the Yes button to display the next task.

After all the tasks have been displayed, you see a message box indicating that you have seen all tasks matching your search criteria.

Quit Microsoft Project for Now

Save and quit Microsoft Project

1   From the File menu, choose Exit.

2   Choose the Yes button if you see the message box asking whether you want to save your work.

3   **Important:** Choose the No button if you see a message box asking whether you want to save changes to the VIEW.MPV view file.

Lesson Summary

To	Do this
Change a view name on the View menu	Use the Define Views command in the View menu. Choose the Edit button, and then in the Name box, enter the name you want to appear on the menu.
Run a built-in macro	From the Macro menu, choose the macro you want. If the macro is not on the menu, choose the Define Macros command from the Macro menu. Then select the macro you want from the list in the Macros box.
Assign a command to a button on the tool bar	Hold down CTRL and click on the Hammer button on the tool bar. In the dialog box, choose the command you want assigned from the list. Select a picture for your button from the Picture Library.

For more information, see in the *Microsoft Project User's Reference*

Macros   227

Tool Bar   561

For an online lesson, see in the Microsoft Project for Windows Online Tutorial

Changing the Look

Printing Views and Reports

Part 5   Review & Practice

Before you begin planning a project of your own, practice the skills you learned in Part 5 by working through the printing and customizing activities in this Review & Practice section. In this practice exercise, you address the communication needs of your project.

Scenario

Now that the Annual Report project is under way and you have learned how to track its progress, many people are interested in getting information about the status of the project. As the project manager, you are expected to provide accurate and timely information to team members and management. Use Microsoft Project's ability to print views and reports to present the information you want in the way you want it.

You will review and practice how to:

- Customize the Gantt Chart view.
- Create a new table.
- Create a new report.

Estimated practice time: 30 minutes

Before You Begin

1   Open the scenario project called 5ANNUAL.MPP.

2   Save the project file as ANNUAL5.MPP.

3   In the Project Information dialog box, change the current date to 8/14/92 8:00 A.M. to match the reports in this scenario.

This project file should look similar to the file you saved after completing the steps in the Part 4 Review & Practice. The timescale has been changed, however, so that the Gantt Chart fits on two pages.

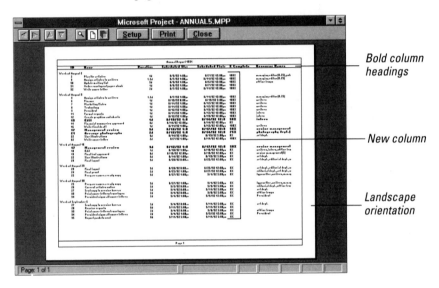

Bold column headings

New column

Landscape orientation

Step 1: Customize the Gantt Chart

The head of investor relations would like a report on the current status of the annual report project. You'd like to show graphically what has been accomplished so far and what is left to do, so printing a Gantt Chart view of the project is the fastest and easiest solution.

Before you print, use the Palette command to specify information to be displayed on each end of some of the Gantt bars according to the table below. Be sure to scroll all the way to the right in the Palette dialog box to see the columns for Left Text and Right Text.

Tasks	Left Text	Right Text
Milestones	Predecessors	Successors
Summary	Scheduled Start date	Scheduled Finish date

Change the Pattern for the non-critical tasks to be a clear box (no fill pattern.) Then, change the header in the Page Setup dialog for the Gantt Chart so it is presentation-quality, as shown in the following print preview.

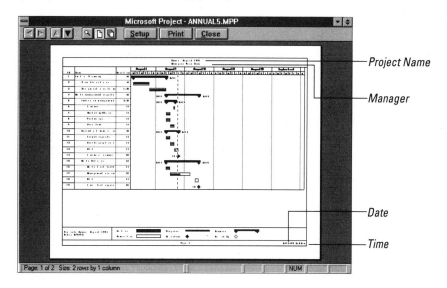

Also, insert a page break above task 20 to balance the number of tasks on each page.

For more information on	See
Printing views and reports	Lesson 16

Step 2: Customize a Table

Although the Entry table gives you basic task information, you are frequently asked to describe the status of tasks in progress. To help you focus on these tasks, create a new table that includes the percent complete of each task. Start by creating a copy of the Entry table. Then replace the Predecessor field with the % Complete field. Name this new table "Progress." From the Task Sheet view, apply the new Progress table.

For more information on	See
Customizing tables	Lesson 17

Step 3: Create a New Report

After using the Progress table to prepare for meetings, you've discovered that it would make a useful report in status meetings. Create a new report based on the Period Task Report and the Progress table you created.

Begin by making a copy of the Periodic Task Report and naming the new report "Periodic Task Progress." In the Periodic Report Definition dialog box, specify the In Progress filter and the Progress table. Be sure the Highlight box is checked. Choose the Text button, and then indicate that you want the column headings and any high-lighted text formatted in bold.

Finally, change the orientation to Landscape in the Page Setup dialog box for this new report so that all the columns fit on one page. If the report still does not fit on one page, you might need to adjust the width of individual columns. Use the report example at the beginning of this Review & Practice as a guide.

For more information on	See
Customizing reports	Lesson 17

Step 4: Create a New View File

Other project managers throughout Victory Sports have heard about your new report and table. In fact, they are becoming a new corporate standard. To share your customizations, save these changes to a new view file called PRGRSSBS.MPV. In the Define Views dialog box, choose the Save button. Then enter the new name.

For more information on	See
Customizing views and view files	Lesson 18

Return to the Task Entry view and save your project

Save button

1   From the View menu, choose Task Entry to prepare for the next lesson.

2   Click the Save button on the tool bar.

If You Want to Continue to the Next Lesson

Close your project file

▶   From the File menu, choose Close.

If You Want to Quit Microsoft Project for Now

Quit Microsoft Project

▶   From the File menu, choose Exit.

Appendixes

Using PERT Charts

This appendix is a lesson in which you'll learn how to use the PERT Chart to get a graphical view of the dependencies between tasks in your project. After you add a task on the PERT Chart, you will change the layout and format of the PERT Chart. In the new format, you will learn how to assign resources to tasks. Finally, using the Task PERT Chart, you will view task predecessors and successors.

You will learn how to:

- View a PERT Chart of the project.
- Add a task on the PERT Chart.
- Change the layout and format of the PERT Chart.
- Use the PERT Chart to assign resources to tasks.
- Display task predecessors and successors.

Estimated lesson time: 30 minutes

Start Microsoft Project

If you closed Microsoft Project in the last lesson, you need to restart the application before you can continue.

▶   Double-click the Microsoft Project icon.

Start the lesson

Do the following to open the project file called PRACTXA.MPP and rename it MOVEXA.MPP.

1   From the File menu, choose Open.

2   In the Directories box, double-click PRACTICE.

3   In the File Name box, double-click PRACTXA.MPP.

4   From the File menu, choose Save As.

5   In the File Name box, type **MOVEXA.MPP**

6   Choose the OK button.

Microsoft Project stores your project on your hard disk with the filename MOVEXA.MPP.

Understanding PERT Chart Basics

A PERT Chart represents each task as a box called a *node*. In the node you can see up to five fields of information. The default node fields are task name, task ID number, duration, scheduled start date, and scheduled finish date. The lines connecting the nodes reflect the task relationships.

You can view the PERT Chart in a view by itself by pressing SHIFT when you choose PERT Chart from the View menu. A full-screen view allows you to see more of your project on the screen at once. On the other hand, you can combine the PERT Chart view with the Task Form in a combination view to conveniently change task details.

The *borders* around each node indicate whether the node is a summary task, a task, or a milestone, and whether or not it is on the critical path. By default, nodes on the critical path have a thick red or patterned border; noncritical nodes have a thin black border; summary tasks have a shadow box border; and milestones have a double or frame border. The PERT Chart in the following illustration displays the different borders for the different types of tasks.

Use the scroll bars to move around the PERT Chart and click a node or node field to select it.

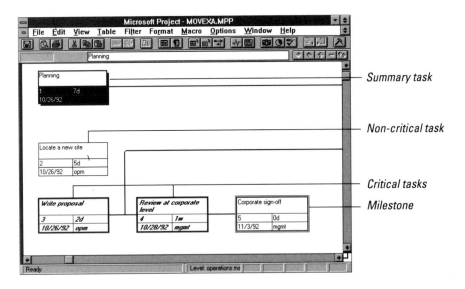

Entering Task Information in a PERT Chart

There are three ways in which you can enter task information in a PERT Chart. You can type directly in the node fields, use the Task Edit Form dialog box, or enter data in the other view of a PERT Chart combination view, such as the Task Form.

You can also double-click on a node to display the Task Edit Form dialog box. Use this technique when you want to enter task information not currently displayed in the node fields; for example, when you have zoomed out the view and the nodes contain only ID numbers.

View the PERT Chart

The branch manager wants an overview of the company move. Make a few last-minute changes and then create a PERT Chart to show at the briefing. Because you need information on potential delays, take a moment to review the critical path of the project.

1   From the View menu, choose PERT Chart.

The PERT Chart appears above the Task Form.

2   Click and drag down on the border between the top and bottom views, to display more of the PERT Chart.

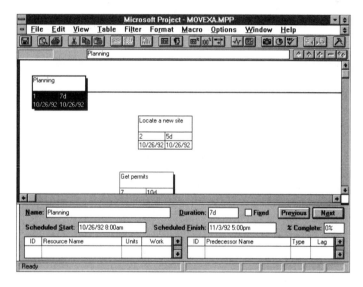

3   Use the scroll arrows to move through the PERT Chart, looking for tasks on the critical path. These tasks have a thick border.

Adjust the node size

To see even more of the PERT Chart, the Zoom Out command on the Format menu lets you reduce node size. Even though you see only the task ID number, you can still make changes to a PERT Chart that is zoomed out. To return the nodes to normal size, use the Zoom In command on the Format menu.

1   Drag the scroll box to the top of the vertical scroll bar.

2   Drag the scroll box all the way to the left on the horizontal scroll bar.

3   Click the task called "Planning."

4 From the Format menu, choose Zoom Out to see an overview of the PERT Chart.

The PERT Chart size is reduced. When the nodes are small, the task ID numbers replace the task names.

Your reduced PERT Chart looks like the following illustration.

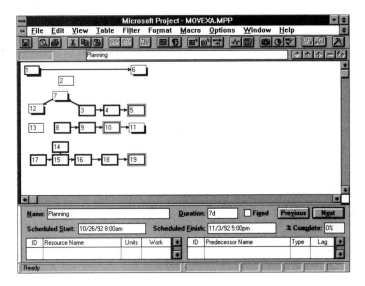

Adding and Deleting Nodes

You can create a new node by dragging the mouse on a blank area of the PERT Chart. You can also use the Insert command on the Edit menu. A new node appears to the right of the selected node. Use the Layout Now command on the Format menu to align the new node with the existing ones.

To delete a node, select it and press DEL or use the Delete command on the Edit menu. If you delete a summary task, the subordinate tasks are also deleted. If you delete a task that has links to other tasks, the relationships are adjusted.

Add a task to the chart

You need to schedule one day to clean up the office area before the move is complete. Insert a task near the end of the project after task 17, "Reconnect computers."

1 From the Format menu, choose Zoom In to see the tasks in detail.

2 From the Edit menu, choose Go To.

3 In the ID box, type **17**

4 Choose the OK button.

5 From the Edit menu, choose Insert.

A new node with the task ID 18 appears.

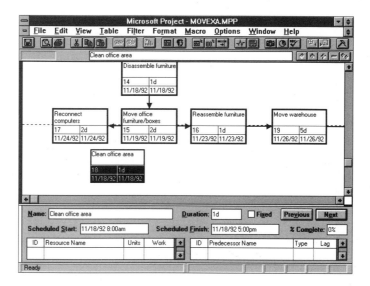

To enter task information, starting typing. The text you enter appears immediately in the entry bar.

6   Type **Clean office area**

Because the task has a duration of one day, you don't need to change the default duration.

7   Click the enter box on the entry bar or press ENTER.

Move a task

To place a task exactly where you want it, click on its border and drag it to a new location.

1   Click and drag the border of task 18.

2   Drag it to below task 17 and release the mouse button.

Adding and Deleting Relationships

To create relationships between nodes, you can drag from the predecessor task to the successor task. When you click and drag from *inside* the node, you establish a finish-to-start relationship, with no lag.

To change the relationship type, or add lead or lag time, double-click the line between the two nodes and enter the new information in the Task Dependency dialog box.

To remove a relationship between two nodes, double-click the line between them and choose the Delete button in the Task Dependency dialog box.

Assign relationships for the new task

Make "Reconnect computers" the predecessor task to "Clean office area," and the "Move complete" milestone the successor.

1 Click and drag from "Reconnect computers" to "Clean office area."

A connecting line appears between the two nodes, and the scheduled start and finish dates for "Clean office area" are now calculated.

2 Click and drag from "Clean office area" to "Move complete."

As you drag to the right, the PERT Chart scrolls to show the other parts of the project. A connecting line appears between the two nodes.

Remove a relationship

Realizing that the "Clean office" task should not be a predecessor for the "Move complete" milestone, you can delete the relationship between these two tasks.

1 Double-click the line connecting the two nodes.

2 In the Task Dependency dialog box, choose the Delete button.

The predecessor relationship between "Clean office area" and "Move complete" has just been deleted.

Save button

Save the project

▶ Click the Save button on the tool bar.

Improving the PERT Chart Layout

By clicking and dragging on a node border, you can place the node where you want it. By holding down SHIFT and dragging a node, you can move the node and its successors or a summary node and its subordinate tasks.

With the Layout Now command on the Format menu, Microsoft Project rearranges the PERT Chart with tasks grouped by outline level.

You can use the Undo Layout command on the Edit menu to restore your previous layout. In addition, the Format menu contains commands you use to change the appearance of nodes in the PERT Chart. With the Text, Borders, Palette, and Layout commands, you can customize the PERT Chart display.

Align new node

To align your new task with others on the critical path, you can use the Layout Now command. To see the effect of the next steps better, use the Zoom Out command. The see the effect even more clearly, make the PERT Chart full-screen.

1 From the Format menu, choose Zoom Out.

2 Hold down the SHIFT key, and from the View menu, choose PERT Chart.

3   From the Format menu, choose Layout Now.

The PERT Chart displays the beginning of the project.

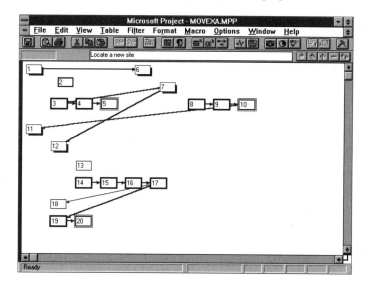

Move a task

To place a task exactly where you want it, click on its border and drag it to a new location.

1   Click and drag the border of task 2.

2   Drag it to under task 1 and release the mouse button.

Change the layout options

You can use the Layout command on the Format menu to change the appearance of the dependency lines from straight to right-angle.

1   From the Format menu, choose Layout.

2   Under Links, select the option button on the right indicating nodes are to be connected with right-angle lines.

3   Clear the Show Arrows check box to remove the arrow heads.

4   Choose the OK button.

The arrow heads are removed from the lines. Note the right-angle lines connecting the summary tasks to the noncritical tasks.

Your project looks like the following illustration.

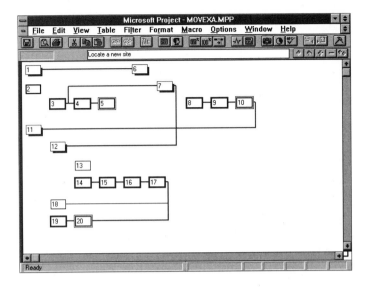

Save button

Save the project

▶ Click the Save button on the tool bar.

Change a field displayed in the nodes

You can use the Palette command on the Format menu to change the fields displayed in nodes. In addition to changing any of the five fields displayed, you can change the node size or use gridlines or cross marks to indicate progress.

Replace the Scheduled Finish date field with a field to display resource initials. Changes you make apply to all nodes in the PERT Chart.

1   From the Format menu, choose Zoom In.

2   Double-click the chart outside the nodes.

The Palette dialog box appears.

3   In the bottom right, click the arrow in the box labeled Field 5 to display the list of field choices.

4   Select Resource Initials from the list.

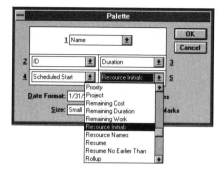

5   Choose the OK button.

Each node displays resource initials in its lower-right field.

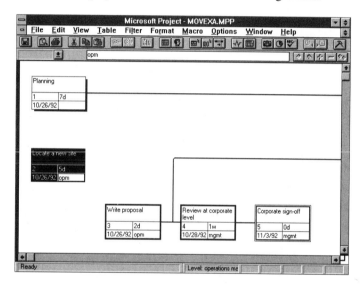

Assigning Resources in a PERT Chart

After adding the resource initials field to the fields displayed in nodes, you can assign resources to tasks directly on the PERT Chart. You simply edit the Resources Initials field in the node for the task to which you want a resource assigned.

Assign a resource to a task in the PERT Chart

Because you are going to be involved in selecting the new site, assign yourself as operations manager to this task.

1   Click in the lower right field of task 2.

2   Type **opm**

3   Click the enter box on the entry bar or press ENTER.

The status bar displays a message indicating that the operations manager is overallocated. You can continue with the rest of this lesson without dealing with this situation right now. However, if you want to learn how to resolve a resource overallocation conflict such as this one, see Lesson 11, "Resource Workloads."

Using the Task PERT Chart

The Task PERT Chart is a version of the PERT Chart that shows the immediate predecessors and successors of the selected task. The Task PERT Chart displays relationship types, such as finish-to-start (FS), and lead or lag time next to the connecting lines. By viewing the PERT Chart and the Task PERT Chart together, you can see the project as a whole, as well as the relationships to the selected task. The Task PERT Chart is especially useful when used with another task view, like the Task Form.

View task relationships in detail

The Task PERT Chart makes it easy to view all the relationships to a single task and identify relationship types. Combine the PERT Chart and Task PERT Chart views and note the relationships on the Task PERT Chart in the bottom window when you select different tasks.

1   Hold down the SHIFT key, then open the View menu and choose Task PERT.

The Task PERT Chart displays the task selected in the top view, with predecessors to the left and successors to the right.

2   Select different tasks in the PERT Chart, such as task 19, "Move warehouse."

Observe how the Task PERT Chart changes.

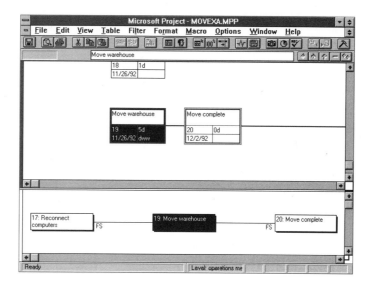

Save button

Save the project

▶   Click the Save button on the tool bar.

One Step Further

A presentation-quality PERT Chart can help you "sell" your project proposal ideas to others. Try the Text and Borders commands on the Format menu to see how you can improve the look of your PERT Chart.

1   From the Format menu, choose Text.

2   In the Item To Change box, select Critical Milestone.

This changes only text in milestones on the critical path.

3   Select the Bold and the Italic check boxes.

4   Choose the OK button.

Your PERT Chart displays the new formats.

You can also format the borders of your PERT Chart.

1   From the Format menu, choose Borders.

Because Critical is already selected in the Item To Change box, you don't need to select it.

2   In the Style box, select Marquee.

3   In the Color box, select any color you want.

4   Choose the OK button.

Note   The view file called PERTS.MPV (in \WINPROJ\LIBRARY on your hard disk) contains several useful PERT-related views and effective presentation formats. To see these views for yourself, open the PERTs view file using the Define Views command from the View menu. The PERTs view file is one of the sample view files supplied with Microsoft Project. See Lesson 18, "Customizing Views," to get more information about opening and using the sample view files.

If You Want to Quit Microsoft Project for Now

Save and quit Microsoft Project

1   From the File menu, choose Exit.

2   Choose the Yes button if you see the message box asking whether you want to save your work.

Lesson Summary

To	Do this
View a PERT Chart of the project	Use the PERT Chart command on the View menu. Press SHIFT before selecting the View menu to get a full-screen display of the PERT Chart.
Add a task on the PERT Chart	Click and drag a rectangle in the location where you want the new node to be.
Display task predecessors and successors	Use the Task PERT Chart command on the View menu.
Use the PERT Chart to assign resources to tasks	Use the Palette command on the Format menu to display the Resource Name or Resource Initials field in the nodes. Then click in the field to enter a resource.
Change the layout of the PERT Chart	Use the Layout Now command on the Format menu to have Microsoft Project arrange the node by summary and subordinate tasks. Use the Layout command on the Format menu to change the appearance of the connecting lines.
Change the format of the PERT Chart	Use the Text commands in the Format menu to change the appearance of text on the PERT Chart. Use the Borders commands in the Format menu to change the appearance of the node border on the PERT Chart.

For more information, see in the *Microsoft Project User's Reference*

For an online lesson, see in the Microsoft Project for Windows Online Tutorial

Preserving and Restoring Custom Settings

This appendix contains instructions for resetting selections in the Preferences dialog box to ensure results that match these lessons. For example, if you have changed the date format, your screen does not look like the screens shown in some of the lessons.

This appendix also contains instructions for returning view and calendar files back to their original state as they were when Microsoft Project was first installed on your computer. Also included are the procedures for protecting your customized files from the changes you make to them as a result of completing the lessons in this book.

In addition, Lessons 18 and 19 depend on your having completed the previous lessons successfully. "Merging View Files" in this appendix includes instructions for merging the elements you need to complete the lesson if you are doing them out of order.

Returning Preferences Back to Default

Before you return the settings in the Preferences dialog box to their original state, it is a good idea to note the current settings. When you have finished the lessons in this book, you can more easily set them back to your own preferences if you note the current settings before following these steps.

Advanced users   All of the settings in the Preferences dialog box are stored in the file called WINPROJ.INI, located in the WINPROJ directory. By copying this file to a different name before following these instructions, you do not have to manually reset them to your own preferences when you are ready to return to your own projects.

Reset the Preferences dialog box

1   From the Options menu, choose Preferences.

2   Choose the Reset button.

3   Choose the OK button.

Protecting View and Calendar Files

Follow these steps only if you want to protect any extensive changes you have made to the default view and calendar files.

Rename your default view file

1   From the View menu, choose Define Views.

2   Choose the Save button.

3 With the view file VIEW.MPV still highlighted, change the extension to SBS.

4 Choose the OK button.

5 Choose the Close button.

Restoring VIEW.MPV to its Original State

To return the view file VIEW.MPV to its original "out-of-the-box" state, you first open the view file called BACKUP.MPV. Then you immediately save it with the name VIEW.MPV. This writes over your customized VIEW.MPV file, but because you made a copy of it in the previous step, you can restore your customized views whenever you want.

Open BACKUP.MPV

1 From the View menu, choose Define Views.

2 Choose the Open button.

3 In the Directories box, double-click WINPROJ.

4 In the File Name box, select BACKUP.MPV.

5 Choose the OK button.

6 When you see the message asking you whether you want to replace or merge BACKUP.MPV with VIEW.MPV, make sure "replace" is selected and choose the OK button.

7 Choose the Close button.

Save BACKUP.MPV as VIEW.MPV

Do the following to copy the contents of BACKUP.MPV over VIEW.MPV. Remember that BACKUP.MPV still remains available.

1 From the View menu, choose Define Views.

2 Choose the Save button.

3 With the view file BACKUP.MPV still highlighted, change the file name to VIEW.MPV.

4 Choose the OK button.

5 When you see the message asking you to confirm that you want to replace VIEW.MPV, choose the OK button.

6 Choose the Close button.

Restoring Your Customized View File

After you complete a lesson and want to work with other projects that use your customized views, you need to reinstate your customized view file. Follow these instructions to open your customized view file, and then rename it VIEW.MPV.

Open VIEW.SBS

1   From the View menu, choose Define Views.

2   Choose the Open button.

3   In the File of Type box, select All files (*.*).

4   In the File Name box, select VIEW.SBS.

5   Choose the OK button.

6   When you see the confirmation message, choose the Yes button.

7   Choose the Close button.

Save VIEW.SBS as VIEW.MPV

Do the following to copy the contents of VIEW.SBS over VIEW.MPV. Remember that VIEW.SBS still remains available.

1   From the View menu, choose Define Views.

2   Choose the Save button.

3   With the view file VIEW.SBS highlighted, change the file name to VIEW.MPV.

4   Choose the OK button.

5   When you see the message asking you to confirm that you want to replace VIEW.SBS, choose the YES button.

6   Choose the Close button.

Protecting Your Calendar File

Follow these instructions if you have changed the calendar. The procedure for renaming, opening, and copying calendar files is similar to the procedure for protecting your view file.

Rename your default calendar file

1   From the Options menu, choose Base Calendars.

2   Choose the Save button.

3   With the calendar file CALENDAR.MPC still highlighted, change the extension to SBS.

4   Choose the OK button.

5   Choose the Close button.

If you have not made any changes to the calendar file, CALENDAR.MPC does not appear in the File Name box, and these restoration procedures do not apply.

Restoring CALENDAR.MPC to its Original State

To return the calendar file CALENDAR.MPC to its original "out-of-the-box" state, you open and edit the calendar file, deleting any of the additional base calendars you might have made. Finally, you edit the base calendar called Standard and reset it to its original state.

Open CALENDAR.MPC

1   From the Options menu, choose Base Calendars.

2   Choose the Open button.

3   From the File Name box, select CALENDAR.MPC.

4   Choose the OK button.

Edit CALENDAR.MPC

Do the following to delete each individual calendar and reset the base calendar called Standard.

1   Select any calendar (except the one called Standard) and choose the Delete button.

2   When you see the confirmation box, choose Yes.

     Repeat steps 1 and 2 until all base calendars (except the one called Standard) are deleted.

3   Select the base calendar called Standard.

4   Choose the Edit button.

5   In the Edit Calendar dialog box, choose the Reset button.

6   When you see the confirmation box, choose Yes.

7   Choose the OK button.

8   Choose the Close button.

     The Calendar file now contains the same information as it did when Microsoft Project was first installed on your computer.

Restoring Your Customized Calendar File

After you complete a lesson and want to work with other projects that use your customized calendar, you need to reinstate your customized calendar file. Follow these instructions to open your customized calendar file, and then rename it CALENDAR.MPC.

Open CALENDAR.SBS

1   From the Options menu, choose Base Calendars.

2   Choose the Open button.

3 In the File of Type box, select All files (*.*).

4 In the File Name box, select CALENDAR.SBS.

5 Choose the OK button.

6 Choose the Close button.

Save CALENDAR.SBS as CALENDAR.MPC

Do the following to copy the contents of CALENDAR.SBS over CALENDAR.MPC. Remember that CALENDAR.SBS still remains available.

1 From the Options menu, choose Base Calendars.

2 Choose the Save button.

3 With the calendar file CALENDAR.SBS highlighted, change the file name to CALENDAR.MPC.

4 Choose the OK button.

5 When you see the message asking you to confirm that you want to replace CALENDAR.SBS, choose the YES button.

6 Choose the Close button.

Merging View Files

Lessons 18 and 19 require that you have created specific elements in your view file from the previous lessons. If you are doing these lessons out of order, you need to do the following to merge these elements from another view file called SBSMORE.MPV.

1 From the View menu, choose Define Views.

2 Choose the Open button.

3 In the File Name box, select SBSMORE.MPV.

4 In the Open View File dialog box, click the Merge from SBSMORE.MPV option.

5 In the Include box, click the option to merge in the elements you need to complete the lesson. Consult the following table to determine which elements to merge into your view file.

6 Choose the OK button.

7 Choose the Close button.

For this lesson	Merge these elements
Lesson 18	Tables
Lesson 19	Tables, Views, Reports

Lesson 19 only   Save your new view file as MONTHLY.MPV.

Save your new view file as MONTHLY.MPV

1   In the Define View dialog box, choose the Save button.

2   In the File Name box, type **monthly.mpv**

3   Choose the Close button.

Using Sample View Files

There are eight sample files (plus two view files containing the original views) included with Microsoft Project. These sample view files contain special views, tables, filters, and reports designed to facilitate a specific project management activity. For example, Lesson 18 uses the sample view file called COST.MPV, containing views that are helpful in tracking project costs. This appendix provides a brief description of all the sample view files, as well as suggestions for how you can use them.

Note   You can get additional information about each view, table, filter, and report in each view file in the document called SAMPVIEW.WRI, located in the LIBRARY subdirectory of the Microsoft Project directory (WINPROJ) on your hard disk. You can open this document with the Write program in the Accessories group in Windows. See your *Microsoft Windows User's Guide* for more information about using Write.

To open and use a sample view, you use the Define Views command on the View menu. When you choose the Open button, you can select the view file you want to open. The sample view files are installed in the LIBRARY subdirectory of your Microsoft Project directory (WINPROJ). For convenience, some of the sample view files are also stored in the WINPROJ directory.

View File Name	Description and Contents
BACKUP.MPV (stored in the WINPROJ directory)	Contains the original set of views. To return to this set, just open this view file.
COST.MPV (also stored in WINPROJ)	Contains views that are formatted to display cost information for tasks or resources. The views in the COST.MPV file help you enter and view information associated with costs. This view file also contains four custom reports.
DEFAULT.MPV	Contains the original set of views. To return to this set, just open this view file.
EASY.MPV	Shows examples of how you can change the words in the views and on the View menu to match terms used in your company. The columns included in a table and the wording for every column title are customizable. You can also change the wording for every view name on the View menu. This view file also contains four custom reports.

View File Name	Description and Contents
ENTRY.MPV	Contains a set of views that illustrate several easy-to-use formats for entering and displaying data. Use these views to enter basic information for a new project. Most of the views are Gantt Chart views, showing graphical schedule information. This view file also contains four custom reports.
PERTS.MPV	Contains a set of views that show some of the possibilities for formatting your PERT Chart. PERT Charts are used to show dependencies between tasks graphically.
RESGRAPH.MPV (also stored in WINPROJ)	Contains a set of views that illustrate a variety of formats and information available for the Resource Graph.
RESMGMT.MPV (also stored in WINPROJ)	Contains a set of views designed to help you enter and view information associated with resources and the management of resources. If you are tracking resources, Microsoft Project provides powerful capabilities to help you use your resources efficiently. This view file also contains four custom reports and two custom filters.
ROLLUP.MPV (also stored in WINPROJ)	Shows four ways you can display "rolled up" tasks on the Gantt Chart. Rolling up tasks means that subordinate task information is displayed on the summary task bar. You control what information is rolled up using the *Rollup* field and the Flag fields. For example, by selecting Scheduled Finish dates in the Rollup field, you can see these dates for the subordinate tasks appear on the summary task above. This view file also contains two custom reports and one custom filter.
TRACKING.MPV	Illustrates several formats for tracking progress, work, and cost on your project.

Glossary

Actual data   Refers to either the project schedule or the project costs for tasks that have begun after the project schedule is in effect based on data you provide.

Calendars   Specifications of the days and hours that resources—people and equipment—are available to work. The base calendar applies to all the resources in the project. Resource calendars apply to specific resources.

Clipboard   Area of memory that holds information selected from a document with a Copy or Cut command. The contents of the Clipboard can be examined with the Accessories utility called the Clipboard Viewer.

Constraints   Schedule restrictions placed on individual tasks to affect task start and finish dates.

Control menu   Menu on every window that allows you to minimize, maximize, restore, move, size, close, run, or switch to another application. Accessed by clicking the Control-menu box, which looks like a minus sign (—) in the upper-left corner of a window.

Control Panel   Built-in Windows utility that allows for customizing the Windows environment and printers.

Cost accrual   The designation for how costs are assigned to a task. Costs can accrue at the start of the task or when the task finishes. They can also be prorated, accruing costs as work progresses.

Critical path   A sequence of *critical tasks* in a project.

Critical Path Method (CPM)   The process for determining the start and finish dates for individual tasks, creating a *critical path* for the project.

Critical tasks   Tasks that, if delayed, would result in the delay of the project. Similarly, if the duration of one or more critical tasks is reduced, the project finishes early. Critical tasks are on the *critical path*.

Collapsing   Hiding the detail tasks below a *summary task*, so that only the summary task is visible.

Date line   A dashed vertical line in the Gantt Chart representing either the current date according to your computer's system clock, or the current date entered in the Project Info dialog box.

Demoting   Indenting a task to show a hierarchical relationship to the task above in the task list.

Duration   The amount of time required to complete a task.

Ellipsis   Three dots (**...**) that sometimes appear after a command name on a menu. Used to indicate that choosing the command will display a dialog box.

Expanding   Making visible all the detail tasks below a *summary task*.

Field   An area in a table or form in which specific information about an individual task or resource is entered and displayed. For example, the Name field in the Task Form contains the name of the task. In tables, the fields are aligned in columns with the field name displayed at the top of the column.

File   An application or document supplied with a name, such that it has been stored on a disk. A project file contains the data you create with the Microsoft Project application.

Filters   Utilities that search through your project to find tasks or resources that match the criteria you set. The tasks or resources that match your criteria are displayed or highlighted, so you can focus on the specific information.

Fixed costs   Costs that remain constant no matter how long the task requires.

Fixed-duration scheduling   Type of scheduling in which a specific task duration is independent of resource work. With fixed-duration scheduling, the number of resources has no effect on how long a task takes.

Footer   Text that appears at the bottom of every printed page of a view or report.

Gantt Chart   A graphical representation of the project schedule, containing Gantt bars that represent tasks. The length of a bar corresponds to the task duration.

Header   Text that appears at the top of every printed page of a view or report.

Insertion point   A blinking vertical bar in a text area of the screen that indicates where characters will appear when you type on the keyboard.

Keys   Fields by which you can sort your task list.

Lag time   Amount of delay between the completion of one task and the start of its successor.

Lead time   Amount of overlap between the completion of one task and the start of its successor.

Legend   A graphical representation of the meaning of the symbols and patterns used in a printed view.

Linking   The process by which a task sequence is established.

Macro   A series of commands performed in a sequence initiated with a single command.

Milestone   A task that represents the completion of a major achievement, phase, or measurable goal. A milestones has a duration of zero (0).

Palette   Command on the Format menu that allows you to change the color, patterns, and shapes of the elements on all the graph and chart views (except for a PERT Chart). In a PERT Chart, the Palette allows you to change the fields displayed in the PERT Chart nodes.

PERT Chart   A graphical representation of the relationships between tasks.

Plan data   A term that refers to either the project schedule or the project costs based on the original plan before the project schedule is in effect.

Pointer   A small graphic object that moves around the screen as you move the mouse on your desk. The pointer changes shape in different functional areas of the screen.

Predecessor   A task that must precede another task.

Project   A collection of related activities or steps, performed in a specified sequence for the purpose of meeting a defined, nonroutine goal.

Resource-driven scheduling   Type of scheduling in which the duration, start dates, and finish dates of a task are determined by the number and allocation of resources.

Resources   The people, groups of people, material, equipment, or facilities required to complete a task. The names of all the resources used in a project are stored in the *resource pool*.

Resource leveling   The process of resolving resource conflicts by ensuring that peak usage of a particular resource never exceeds the maximum available amount of that resource.

Scheduled data   A term that refers to either the project schedule or the project costs for future tasks, based on data provided by the user after the project schedule is in effect.

Sorting   Process that changes the order of the tasks, so you can better locate and review the project information you need.

Successor   A task that follows another task.

Summary tasks   General headings with subordinate tasks indented below them. Summary tasks provide an outline structure that identifies the project's major phases. Each level of indenting represents an additional level of detail for the task.

Tasks   The steps in a project.

Timescale   The units of time that represent the displayed project schedule. The timescale contains two units of measurement: the *major* timescale and the *minor* timescale. The major and minor timescales are paired in combinations, such as Months over Weeks, Weeks over Days, and Days over Hours.

Unit   A person, a room, a machine, or whatever constitutes a single resource assigned to a task.

Variable costs   Costs that increase as the task progresses.

View   Any of the various presentation formats used to enter and display project information. Sheet views display task or resource information in rows and columns, as in a spreadsheet. Chart and graph views provide graphical representations of project information. Forms display task or resource information in a format similar to that which you complete with pencil and paper. In combination views, the top part of the screen contains one view, while the bottom part of the screen contains another.

Index

Note: Italicized page numbers refer to illustrations.

A

active view
    changing, 17, 18
    defined, 64
    printing, 76, 77, 199
actual data
    comparing to plan data, 174–75
    defined, 166, 265
    entering, 170–72
    viewing, 172–73
Actual Finish field, 171
Actual Start field, 171
ascending sort order, 86–87, 89
As Late As Possible constraint, 156, 157
As Soon As Possible constraint, 156, 157, 161

B

BACKUP.MPV file
    defined, 263
    opening, 258
    saving as VIEW.MPV, 258
Base Calendar Definition dialog box, 111, 114
base calendars
    assigning resources to, 115–16
    changing, 110–13
    copying, 113
    creating, 113–15
    default, 110
    defined, 110
    new, naming, 115
    printing report, 201
Base Calendars dialog box, 111–12
baselines
    creating, 136
    displaying, 168–69
Best Fit button, 43
borders
    around nodes, 244
    printing, 195
budget, viewing, 149
Button Definition dialog box, 231

C

Calculator button, 231
calendar files
    customized, restoring, 260–61
    renaming default file, 259
CALENDAR.MPC file
    defined, 113
    editing, 260
    opening, 260
    renaming, 259
    restoring, 260
    saving CALENDAR.SBS as, 261
calendars
    assigning resources to, 115–16
    base, defined, 110
    changing to shorten critical path, 183–84
    changing workdays, 110–11, 112–13
    changing working hours, 111–12, 114
    copying, 113
    defined, 265
    and holidays, 116–17
    overview, 110
    reports, 201, 202–3
    resetting, 112
    resource, 110–13, 116
    standard, defined, 110
    types of, 110
CALENDAR.SBS file
    opening, 260–61
    renaming CALENDAR.MPC file as, 259
    saving as MPC file, 261
cancel box, 17
Chart views, 12–13
check boxes, *xxii*
clicking, defined, xxviii
Clipboard
    defined, 265
    using, 38–39
Collapse button, *51*, 57
collapsing
    defined, 265
    tasks, 51–52, 57
colors, changing, 70
column width, changing, 43, 106
combination views, 14–15
command buttons, *xxii*
commands, accessing, xx–xxi
COMMANDS.WRI file, 232
constraint dates, defined, 156
Constraint Dates table, 162–63

Catapult, Inc.

Catapult is a national software training company dedicated to providing the highest quality application software training. Years of PC and Macintosh instruction for major corporations and government institutions provide the models used in building Catapult's exclusive Performance-Based Training program. Based on the principles of adult learning, Performance-Based Training materials ensure that training participants leave the classroom with the ability to apply skills acquired during the training day.

Catapult's Curriculum Development group is pleased to share their training skills with a wider audience through the Step by Step series. Microsoft Project for Windows is the second in the Step by Step series to be produced by Catapult Press. This book and others in the series will help you develop the confidence necessary to achieve increased productivity with your Microsoft products.

Catapult's corporate headquarters are in Bellevue, Washington.

STEP BY STEP SERIES
The Official Microsoft® Courseware

These timesaving, all-in-one book-and-software training packages from Microsoft Press are the official courseware for Microsoft's top-selling software. Each takes a modular approach in teaching users of all levels. All of the lessons are illustrated with examples and are fully integrated with the practice files on disk—ideal for professional training in the classroom or for self-paced learning.

Each lesson includes: ■ clear objectives ■ step-by-step instructions
■ real-world business examples ■ skill-strengthening exercises

Users can supplement and reinforce what they've learned with the shortcuts
and reminders in the practice documents on the accompanying disk.

MICROSOFT® WINDOWS™ 3.1
STEP BY STEP

Catapult, Inc.

Learn Microsoft Windows quickly and easily with
MICROSOFT WINDOWS 3.1 STEP BY STEP.
**296 pages, softcover with one 3.5-inch disk
$29.95 ($39.95 Canada)   Order Code WI31ST**

MICROSOFT® WORD FOR WINDOWS™
STEP BY STEP

Microsoft Corporation

Learn to produce professional-quality documents with ease.
Covers version 2.
**296 pages, softcover with one 5.25-inch disk
$29.95 ($39.95 Canada)   Order Code WD2STM**

MICROSOFT® EXCEL FOR WINDOWS™
STEP BY STEP, 2nd ed.

Microsoft Corporation

Become a spreadsheet expert the easy way!
Covers version 4.0.
**336 pages, softcover with one 3.5-inch disk
$29.95 ($39.95 Canada)   Order Code EXSTP2**

MICROSOFT® EXCEL MACROS
STEP BY STEP

*Steve Wexler and Julianne Sharer
for WexTech Systems, Inc.*

Create effective and efficient macros with Microsoft
Excel version 4.0 for Windows™ and the Apple® Macintosh®.
**272 pages, softcover with two 3.5-inch disks
$34.95 ($47.95 Canada)   Order Code EXMAST**

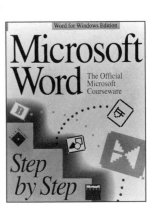

Great Resources from Microsoft Press